Penguin Handbooks
The Penguin Book of Knitting

Pam Dawson was born in 1924. She taught herself to knit at
the age of seven and as an adult took up this hobby
professionally as Assistant to the Resident Designer of a
spinning company. In 1966 she was appointed Assistant
Editor of *Vogue Knitting Book* and in 1970 became a founder
member of the weekly partwork *Golden Hands*. She compiles
the series of 'Golden Hands Specials' and is, at present, the
knitting and crochet editor for *Golden Hands Monthly*. In
1974 Mrs Dawson took part in two programmes for Thames
Television on knitting and crochet, and a year later wrote
Knitting Fashion to accompany the BBC series of television
programmes of the same name.

Pam Dawson lives in London and has two married daughters
and two granddaughters.

PAM DAWSON

The Penguin Book of Knitting

Illustrations by Coral Mula
Photographs (Part Two)
by Margaret Murray

PENGUIN BOOKS

Penguin Books Ltd, Harmondsworth,
Middlesex, England
Penguin Books, 625 Madison Avenue,
New York, New York 10022, U.S.A.
Penguin Books Australia Ltd, Ringwood,
Victoria, Australia
Penguin Books Canada Ltd, 2801 John Street,
Markham, Ontario, Canada L3R 1B4
Penguin Books (N.Z.) Ltd, 182–190 Wairau Road,
Auckland 10, New Zealand

First published in Penguin Books 1978
Reprinted 1978

Made and printed in Great Britain by
Butler & Tanner Ltd, Frome and London
Set in Monophoto Times

Contents

Part One

Part Two

Part One

Introduction

Knitting is one of the oldest handicrafts known to mankind but its scope and range of application is still not fully appreciated. Anything which can be produced by a machine can be hand-knitted and the resultant fabric will be much more attractive – in fact, machines can only copy what has been achieved with this craft since time immemorial.

Machine knitting has taken this craft into the realms of highest fashion but this book is entirely devoted to knitting as a superb handicraft. The emphasis is on the pleasure and satisfaction which can be derived from creating something beautiful and practical with your own hands.

Every knitter automatically combines two skills at one and the same time – that of a weaver and that of a dress maker. The expense incurred with this fascinating hobby is minimal. For the price of a pair of needles and some balls of yarn, you can begin to explore its endless possibilities. It is the purpose of this book to extend your knowledge and enjoyment of the craft, whatever your level of skill as a knitter, either as a complete beginner or experienced devotee.

Throughout this book, each technical chapter will end with a project suitable for either a beginner or more advanced knitter, to encourage knitters to experiment with the methods explained.

Knitting needles

These are the main tools you will require but as you progress you may need to purchase additional items, such as stitch holders, cable needles, needle gauges, blunt-ended sewing needles for making up, and so on.

Knitting needles are sold in pairs in varying sizes and lengths. These sizes were converted to metric measurements in 1976 but the chart shown here gives both the metric size and the old British number for compari-

British	Metric	British	Metric
14	2 mm	5	$5\frac{1}{2}$ mm
13	$2\frac{1}{4}$ mm	4	6 mm
12	$2\frac{3}{4}$ mm	3	$6\frac{1}{2}$ mm
11	3 mm	2	7 mm
10	$3\frac{1}{4}$ mm	1	$7\frac{1}{2}$ mm
9	$3\frac{3}{4}$ mm	0	8 mm
8	4 mm	00	9 mm
7	$4\frac{1}{2}$ mm	000	10 mm
6	5 mm		

Knitting needle sizes British and metric

son. Each needle is shaped at one end, enabling stitches to be worked without splitting the yarn, and has a knob at the other end to prevent the stitches slipping off the needle. Pairs of needles are required for flat knitting in rows.

Sets of four needles, shaped at both ends, are also available for knitting in rounds to produce a circular fabric. These are also sold in various sizes and lengths. Knitting in rounds may also be worked on a circular needle, which has two small rigid needle sec-

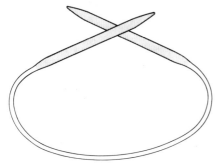

Circular needle

tions shaped at the ends, which are then joined together with a length of flexible nylon. These are sold in various sizes and lengths but can only be used when the

number of stitches cast on is sufficient to reach from one needle point to the other.

Knitting yarns

The yarns available for hand knitting can be made from a variety of fibres, whether natural or man-made, or combinations of both. Each fibre, whatever its eventual composition, goes through many processes, such as twisting and dyeing, before it is made available to the knitter.

Ply

These fibres begin as a single, spun thread of any thickness. Each single thread is then combined with one, two, three or more similar threads to make up the 'ply' of the yarn. Because each single thread is not to any definite thickness, the word 'ply' cannot be taken to refer to a yarn of a specific thickness. Some '2 ply' Shetland yarns can be thicker than a standard '4 ply' yarn.

Twisting

Once the number of strands have been determined to form the final 'ply', the yarn is

Tension	Lengths of Circular Twin Pin Needles and Minimum Number of Stitches Required						
Stitches to 2·5 cm (1 in)	40·5 cm (16 in)	51·0 cm (20 in)	61·0 cm (24 in)	68·5 cm (27 in)	70·6 cm (30 in)	91·5 cm (36 in)	106·5 cm (42 in)
5	80	100	120	135	150	180	210
5½	88	110	132	148	165	198	230
6	96	120	144	162	180	216	250
6½	104	130	156	175	195	234	270
7	112	140	168	189	210	252	294
7½	120	150	180	202	225	270	315
8	128	160	192	216	240	288	336
8½	136	170	204	220	255	306	357
9	144	180	216	243	270	324	378

then twisted in various ways to give it a specific character and convert it into a workable knitting yarn. Without any twist, the yarn easily breaks but the knitters in Iceland prefer untwisted yarn to produce their traditional soft fabrics. The looser the twist, the softer the yarn; very tightly twisted yarns produce hard-wearing, 'crepe' yarns.

Weights

Once a suitable, continuous thread has been produced and dyed by the spinner, it is then formed into balls or hanks of yarn for sale to the public. Each ball contains a specific metric weight and yarn is not normally sold by length. The density of dye used to produce a certain colour can sometimes affect the final weight of the yarn. Also, all pure wool yarns have to retain a certain moisture content, otherwise they become too brittle to handle. These factors can have an overall effect on the weight of each yarn, even within the same range, so that each ball may contain a different length of yarn.

The ball of yarn is then secured with a ball band, which will give details of the weight in grammes, the composition of the yarn, the ply, details of colour and dye lot numbers and washing, dry-cleaning and pressing codes. Always keep a ball band when you begin to knit, so that you can

---

The code basically consists of four symbols:

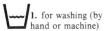 1. for washing (by hand or machine)

 3. for ironing

 2. for bleaching

 4. for dry cleaning

The symbols are always presented in the same sequence. In the UK they are mainly found arranged vertically; in other European countries they are more usually arranged horizontally.

 Washing

 Do not machine wash

 Do not wash

Washing Temperatures

100°C	Boil	Self-explanatory.
95°C	Very hot	Water heated to near boiling temperature.
60°C	Hot	Hotter than the hand can bear. The temperature of water coming from many domestic hot taps.
50°C	Hand-hot	As hot as the hands can bear.
40°C	Warm	Pleasantly warm to the hand.
30°C	Cool	Feels cool to the touch.

 Bleaching

This symbol indicates that household (chlorine) bleach could be used. Care must be taken to follow the manufacturer's instructions.

 When this symbol appears on a label household bleach must *not* be used.

 Ironing

The number of dots in the ironing symbol indicates the correct temperature setting – the fewer the dots the cooler the iron setting.

cool	warm	hot	do not iron

 Dry cleaning

The letter in the circle refers to the solvent which may be used in the dry cleaning process, and those using coin-operated dry cleaning should check that the cleaning symbol shown on the label is the same as that in the instructions given on the front of the machine.

 Goods normal for dry cleaning in all solvents.

Goods normal for dry cleaning in perchloroethylene, white spirit, Solvent 113 and Solvent 11.

Goods normal for dry cleaning in white spirit or Solvent 113.

 Do not dry clean.

Codes compiled by the Home Laundering Consultative Council

check all this information. If you require an additional ball to complete a garment you will then be able to quote the colour and dye lot number. Although dyeing is a very carefully regulated process, there can be a slight difference in each dye lot.

When a garment is completed, you will also need to know whether it can be machine washed, dry cleaned and, most important of all, whether the yarn should be pressed. The chart shown here giving the symbols and their meanings has been compiled by the Home Laundering Consultative Council.

Reading a knitting pattern

Materials

If you are going to work from a published pattern, it is important to realize that the design will have been based on a specific yarn and needle size. If you use another yarn the finished fabric may not look exactly the same and you may need a different quantity of yarn.

Headings

Each pattern is set out in separate sections; the materials required, the overall sizes, the tension (see Chapter 3), the working instructions for each section and the final making up details.

Abbreviations

Because of the length of knitting instructions and the limited space available in a leaflet or magazine, all knitting terms are abbreviated into a form of shorthand. The general abbreviations used in the instructions will be given in full as a separate section in

the pattern. These terms can differ from one publication to another, so always check this section carefully.

When an unusual knitting method is being used to form a pattern, as with Aran stitches, the working method is described in full when it is first used in the instructions and will then be given an abbreviated term, which will be used throughout the rest of the pattern.

The general abbreviations used throughout this book are shown on page 143.

Sizes

Most knitting designs are given in more than one size to ensure that the knitter has the widest possible choice. The first set of figures in the instructions will always refer to the smallest size. The figures relating to each subsequent size will then either be shown in square brackets, [ ], or printed in *italics*. The second size will therefore be shown as the first set of figures in square brackets, or italics, and so on for each respective size. When only one set of figures is given, it refers to all sizes. It is as well to read right through a pattern before beginning to knit and underline all the figures which apply to the size you are making.

Tension

This section is so vital that it is fully explained in Chapter 3. Whether you are a complete beginner or an experienced knitter, it is essential that you understand the important part which tension plays in all designing.

Measuring

When measuring the length of a section, the knitting should be laid on a flat surface and measured in the centre of the piece, using

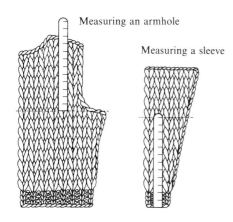

Measuring an armhole

Measuring a sleeve

either a metal tape or rigid rule. Never measure round a curve, such as an armhole, or on the side edge of a shaped section, such as a sleeve.

Notes

A set of instructions will sometimes contain an unusual working method, such as using two strands of yarn throughout. Your attention will be drawn to this fact by means of a separate heading, 'Note', in the instructions.

Project for experienced knitters

Experimenting with yarn and stitches

Afghan rug

Each square will take approximately 15–20 g.

Using the correct needle size, cast on the number of stitches to give a square 20 cm wide (see Chapter 3), and work with any yarns of a double knitting quality, in as many colours as required for a length of 20 cm. Adjusting the number of stitches when necessary to give correct multiples, work in any of the patterns given in this book and make a total of 48 squares.

Join 6 squares together to form one row and make a total of 8 rows, to give a rug measuring 120 cm wide by 160 cm long. Trim top and bottom edges with fringes (see Chapter 10).

Afghan rug

15

2

How to begin

All knitted fabrics are formed by a series of interlocking stitches, one above the other, in rows or rounds.

To begin to knit you need to know four basic steps – how to cast on the loops which form the foundation row of the fabric; how to knit or purl each stitch and how to securely fasten off each stitch at the end of a section of fabric, by means of casting off.

Once you have mastered these very simple steps, the world of knitting is at your fingertips.

Holding the yarn and needles

Knitting is a most relaxing hobby and the real secret is to find a way of holding the yarn and needles which comes easily and naturally to you. The following suggestions are a guide to right-handed knitters. Left-handers should hold the figure up to. a mirror.

One of a pair of needles is held in the right hand to make the stitches and the other is used in the left hand, to hold the completed stitches.

The yarn should be wound round the fingers of the right hand in such a way that it flows evenly over the fingers to create a firm fabric.

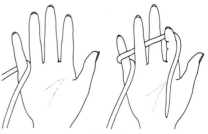

Winding yarn round right hand

Casting on

There are many different methods of casting on but each version begins with a slip loop on the left-hand needle.

How to hold a pair of needles

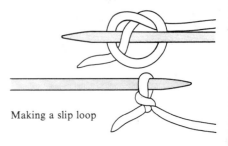

Making a slip loop

16

Casting on with two needles

Put the point of the needle in your right hand into the slip loop from front to back, take the yarn under and over this point and pull the yarn through the slip loop to make a stitch. Put the new stitch on to the left-hand needle. *Put the point of the right-hand needle between the two loops on the left-hand needle from front to back, take the yarn under and over this point and pull the yarn through on to the needle to make another stitch. Put the new stitch on to the left-hand needle. Continue in this way from the point marked with an * until the required number of stitches is on the left-hand needle.

A looser version of this method can be obtained by working into each new loop on the left-hand needle, instead of between the loops.

Casting on with one needle

Only one needle is required for this version, as the thumb of the left hand replaces the

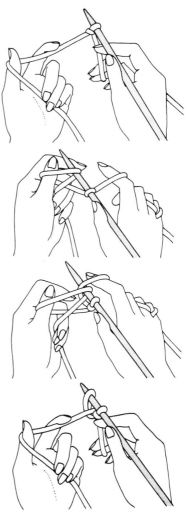

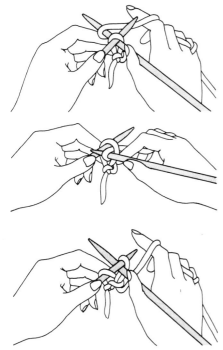

Casting on with two needles

Casting on with one needle

17

left-hand needle. Make a slip loop and place this on the needle, leaving an end approximately 40 cm long, which will be sufficient to make about twenty-five stitches. Hold the needle in the right hand, then place the short end of yarn between the index finger and thumb of the left hand, take it round the thumb and across the palm, holding it down with the third finger. *Put the point of the needle under the loop round the thumb, take the other end of yarn from the main ball under and over this point and pull the yarn through the loop on the thumb to make a stitch. Leave this stitch on the needle, tighten it by pulling up the short end of yarn, then take the short end round the thumb again, ready to make the next stitch. Continue in this way from the point marked with an * until you have made the required number of stitches.

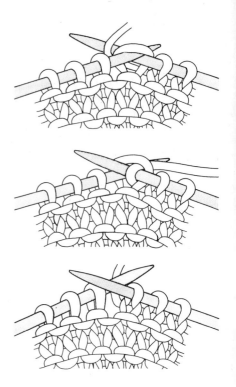

Knitting and purling

Knitted stitches

These two stitches form the basis of all knitted fabrics, however complicated they may appear.

Knitted stitches

Having cast on the stitches, hold this needle in the left hand and the empty needle in the right hand. *Put the point of the right-hand needle into the first stitch on the left-hand needle from front to back, keep the yarn at the back of the work throughout and take it under and over this point and pull the yarn through. Leave the new stitch on the right-hand needle and drop the stitch from the left-hand needle. Continue in this way from the point marked with an * until all the cast on stitches have been transferred to the right-hand needle.

Change the needle holding the stitches to the left hand to work the next row and repeat from the * to the end of the row.

Knitting each row in this way is referred to as 'garter stitch'.

Purled stitches

Hold the needles as given for knitted stitches. *Put the point of the right-hand needle into the first stitch on the left-hand needle from right to left, keep the yarn at the front of the work throughout and take it over and round this point and pull the yarn through. Leave the new stitch on the

18

Garter stitch

Stocking stitch

right-hand needle and drop the stitch from the left-hand needle. Continue in this way from the point marked with an * until all

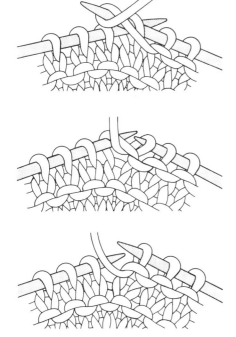

Purled stitches

the stitches have been transferred to the right-hand needle.

Change the needle holding the stitches to the left hand to work the next row and repeat from the * to the end of the row.

Knitting the first row and purling the second row, and continuing to alternate them in this way, is referred to as 'stocking stitch'. The purl side of this fabric is referred to as 'reversed stocking stitch'.

Knitting and purling stitches in the same row

Hold the needles and work the first stitch as given for knitted stitches, *bring the yarn forward between the two needles to the front and purl the next stitch, take the yarn back between the two needles and knit the next stitch. Continue in this way from the point marked with an * until all the stitches have been transferred to the right-hand needle.

Change the needle holding the stitches to the left hand to work the next row, then purl all the stitches which were knitted and knit

Single rib

Moss stitch

all the stitches which were purled on the previous row.

Knitting and purling alternate stitches in this way is referred to as 'single rib'.

To work moss stitch, work the first row as given for single rib but on the next row knit all the knitted stitches and purl all the purled stitches.

Casting off

Once a section has been knitted, it is necessary to bind off each loop on the needle so that it does not unravel. It is important to work each stitch in the correct pattern before casting it off.

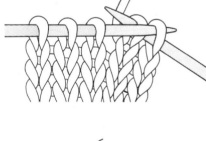

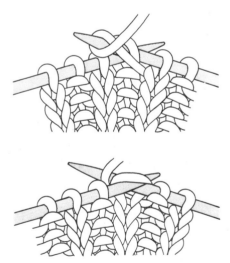

Knitting and purling in the same row

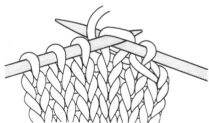

Casting off

Casting off in knitting

Knit the first two stitches on to the right-hand needle in the usual way, *using the point of the left-hand needle lift the first knitted stitch over the second stitch and off the needle, leaving one stitch on the right-hand needle, knit the next stitch on the left-hand needle. Continue in this way from the point marked with an * until one stitch remains on the right-hand needle. Break off

the yarn leaving an end approximately 15 cm long, draw this end through the last stitch and pull it up tightly. This is referred to as 'fasten off'.

Casting off in purling

This is worked exactly as given for casting off in knitting, but each stitch is purled before it is cast off.

Project for beginners

Making a garment from garter stitch squares.

Over-jersey

To fit 86–91 cm bust. Total quantity of yarn required, 700 g of double knitting.

Square

Using 4 mm needles cast on 36 stitches by the thumb method, or the correct number to give 15 cm in width. Work in garter stitch for 15 cm. Cast off loosely.

Using colours as required, make 37 more squares in same way (38 in all). Join together as shown in diagram. Sew underarm and side seams. Do not press.

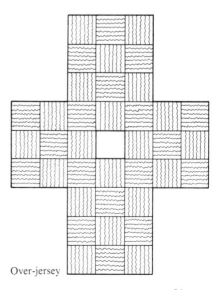

Over-jersey

21

3

Tension and shaping

The craft of knitting combines two separate techniques in producing any garment – that of a weaver and that of a dressmaker. What is referred to as 'tension' controls the structure of the fabric and increasing and decreasing produce the final shape of the garment.

Tension

Apart from mastering the basic steps in knitting, the real skill depends on one simple factor – tension. Unless you appreciate the important part this plays in the structure of knitted fabrics, you cannot hope to achieve satisfactory results from an existing pattern, or begin to experiment for yourself.

In dressmaking, the weaving operation has already been taken into account and one metre in either width or length will be exactly the same, whether the fabric used is a heavyweight tweed or soft silk. This does not apply in knitting, where the type of yarn and needle size used to produce the fabric will determine the number of stitches and rows required to arrive at a given measurement.

Many knitters mistakenly believe that the term 'tension' means achieving an even fabric and if they feel that their knitting is 'average', they can safely dispense with this section. It does, in fact, relate to the number of stitches and rows to a given measure-

ment, usually 10 cm, which the *designer* of the garment has achieved, using the yarn and needle size quoted. It is never safe to assume that you can knit to exactly the same tension and even as little as one stitch more or less in every 10 cm can result in a jersey for an 86 cm bust size being approximately 5 cm too large or too small.

Knitters will very often purchase a different yarn from that given in the instructions. As explained in Chapter 1, the character of each yarn varies considerably and this substitution only adds to the difficulty of obtaining the correct tension.

How to achieve the correct tension

It is vital that both beginners and more experienced knitters should first work a tension sample before commencing any pattern. The tension of the original is given under the appropriate heading in the instructions; if you find you have more stitches and rows to the given measurement, then your tension is too tight and you must change to one size larger needles to overcome this. Too few stitches and rows mean that your tension is too loose and you must change to one size smaller needles. This is no reflection on your knitting skill and it doesn't matter how many times you have to change the needle size to achieve the correct tension, but unless you take the time to check that you can obtain the same tension as the designer, you will never be certain of making a perfect garment.

Where a design is worked from the lower edge to the shoulders in rows or rounds, the number of stitches given in the tension governs the width of the garment and the number of rows determines the length. In this case, the vital figure is the stitch tension, as the number of rows can usually be amended to alter the length. Do make absolutely sure, however, that the pattern is not based on an exact number of rows which cannot be adjusted.

How to check tension

Once you have worked your tension sample in the same yarn, needle size and stitch given in the pattern, place it on a flat surface and secure it at each corner with pins. Lay a firm rule across the knitting and mark out with pins the exact number of stitches you have obtained to the centimetre, then count and mark the rows in the same way. The original tension will have been calculated without pressing or stretching, unless specifically stated in the instructions. If you are satisfied that your tension is accurate, it is safe to begin knitting.

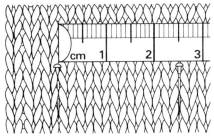

Correct tension giving 7 st to 2·5 cm

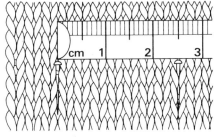

Tension too tight, 7½ st to 2·5 cm

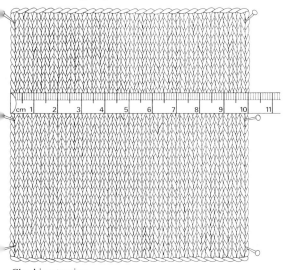

Checking tension

Remember – too many stitches means the tension is too tight; too few stitches means that the tension is too loose.

Shaping

Once you have obtained the correct fabric, each section can then be shaped by either reducing the number of stitches in a row to give less width, or increasing them to give additional width. Casting on and casting off stitches can also be used as a means of increasing or decreasing large groups of stitches.

How to decrease one stitch

One stitch is usually decreased at each end of the same knitted row, to balance the overall shape. This simply means putting the point of the right-hand needle through two stitches, instead of one, and knitting them both together in the usual way. This is referred to as 'knit 2 together' and the decrease will form a stitch slanting to the right.

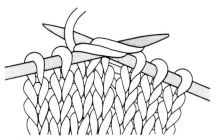

Knit 2 together to decrease one stitch

To decrease a stitch which slants to the left on a knitted row, insert the point of the right-hand needle into the next stitch on the left-hand needle as if to knit it but slip it on to the right-hand needle without working it,

knit the next stitch on the left-hand needle, then with the point of the left-hand needle lift the unworked stitch over the top of the knitted stitch and off the needle. This is

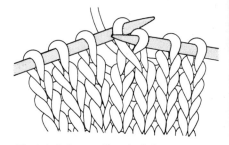

Slip 1, knit 1, pass slipped stitch over to decrease one stitch

referred to as 'slip 1, knit 1, pass the slipped stitch over', and the decreased stitch is not twisted.

An alternative to this method is to put the point of the right-hand needle through the back loops of two stitches and knit them together in the usual way. This is referred to as 'knit 2 together through the back of the loops', but the decreased stitch is twisted.

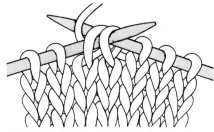

Knit 2 together through the back of the loops to decrease one stitch

Stitches can be decreased on a purl row by purling the stitches instead of knitting them, but 'purl 2 together' will form a stitch slanting to the right on the knitted side. It is very difficult to work the slipped stitch decrease on a purl row but 'purl 2 together through the back of the loops' will produce a twisted stitch slanting to the left on the knitted side.

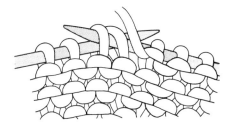

Purl 2 together to decrease one stitch

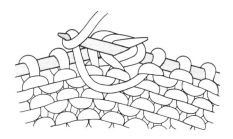

Purl 2 together through the back of the loops to decrease one stitch

All of these methods can be used to work three stitches together, thus decreasing two stitches; on the slip stitch version, slip the first stitch, then knit the next two stitches together before passing the slip stitch over.

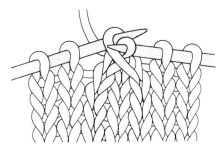

Slip 1, knit 2 together, pass the slipped stitch over to decrease 2 stitches

How to decrease groups of stitches

This method is used for underarm, neck and shoulder shapings; cast off the required number of stitches in the correct pattern and note that the stitch which remains on the right-hand needle after the casting off has been completed is then counted as one of the remaining stitches of the main fabric.

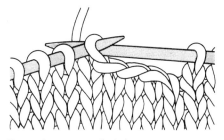

Decreasing groups of stitches

How to increase one stitch

Here again, the stitches should be increased at each end of the same knitted row. Knit the first stitch in the usual way but do not drop it off the left-hand needle. Put the point of the right-hand needle into the back loop of the same stitch and knit another stitch, then let the stitch drop off the left-hand needle. This method of increasing forms a little 'pip' inside the first edge stitch; to give

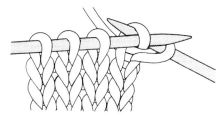

Knit into the front and back of same stitch to increase one

the same effect at the other end of the row, work the increased stitch into the last but one stitch, then knit the last stitch in the usual way.

To avoid a 'pip' at each end, or in the middle of a section where increasing is required on a knitted row, with the point of the right-hand needle pick up the strand of yarn between the last stitch knitted and the next stitch on the left-hand needle, then put this loop on to the left-hand needle. Knit this extra loop through the back to avoid a gap in the fabric.

How to increase groups of stitches

Extra stitches can be cast on at the beginning of a knitted row and each stitch knitted in the usual way to the end of the row. The work can then be turned and the same number of stitches cast on at the beginning of the next row and worked to the end; the shaping is then virtually evenly balanced.

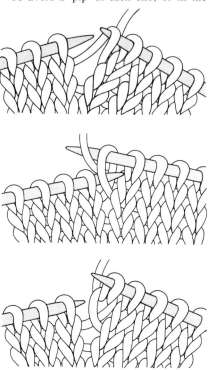

Picking up a loop to increase one

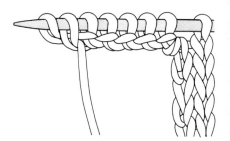

Increasing groups of stitches

Project for beginners

Shaping in garter stitch to form diamonds and triangles.

Scarf

Total quantity of yarn required, 350 g of double knitting.

Diamond

Using 4 mm needles cast on 2 sts and knit 1 row.

2nd row K into the front and back of first st – called Kfb –, K1.

3rd row K3.

4th row (Kfb) twice, K1.
5th row K5.
6th row Kfb, K to last 2 sts, Kfb, K1.
Repeat the 5th and 6th rows until there are 59 sts, then repeat 5th row. **.
Next row K1, K2 tog, K to last 3 sts, K2 tog tbl, K1.
Next row K to end.
Repeat the last 2 rows until 5 sts remain, ending with a K row.
Next row K1, K3 tog, K1.
Next row K3.
Next row K1, K2 tog.
Cast off.

Make 5 more diamonds in same way, varying colours as required.

Triangle

Work as given for diamond to **. Cast off.
Work 13 more triangles in same way, varying colours as required.
Do not press. Join together as shown in diagram. Make four tassels (see Chapter 10), and sew one to each corner.

A = 1st colour
B = 2nd colour
C = 3rd colour

Scarf

4

Circular knitting

Knitting on a pair of needles and turning the work at the end of each row produces what is referred to as 'flat knitting'. Circular knitting, using sets of four needles or a circular needle to work in rounds, has many uses.

This method forms seamless, tubular fabrics, such as socks, or geometric shapes which can be joined together in a variety of ways.

In each case the principle is the same and the final shape of the fabric is controlled by the number of stitches cast on and by increasing and decreasing at given points.

needles into a triangle shape and use the fourth needle to knit across the stitches of the first needle, then once this needle is free use it to work across the stitches of the next needle, and so on.

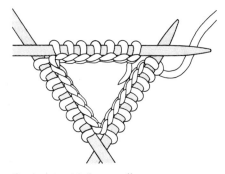

Casting on with four needles

Tubular fabrics

Details of the needles required for this technique have been given in Chapter 1.

Casting on

When casting on with four needles one of the set is used for making the loops and these are divided on to the remaining three needles. Any casting on method may be used but as a beginner it would be easier to use the two-needle version, making the required number of stitches on the first needle, then on the second and third needles, taking care to ensure that they do not become twisted round the needles. Join the three

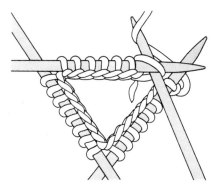

Beginning to knit with the fourth needle

When casting on with a circular needle, first make sure that you will have sufficient stitches to reach from one needle point to the other. Use each shaped section to cast on by the two-needle method.

Working tubular fabrics

The important point to remember in circular knitting is that the right side of the fabric is always facing you. It is as well to mark the beginning of the round with a loop of contrasting yarn as it is easy to lose track. Make a slip loop in the contrast yarn and place it on the first needle to mark the start of the round, then slip the loop from one needle to the other on every round without knitting it.

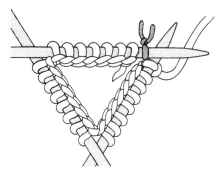

Marking beginning of round

The basic stitches are very simple in circular knitting; to produce stocking stitch every round is knitted; to produce garter stitch alternate rounds are knitted and purled throughout; to produce ribbed fabric each knitted stitch is knitted and each purled stitch is purled on every round.

Casting off is worked in the usual way, keeping the pattern correct.

Flat geometric shapes

These are easier to work from the centre of the shape outwards, beginning with a few cast on stitches and a set of four or five needles, using the two-needle method to make the loops. Any geometric shape can be produced by working to the outer edge and increasing at certain points on every alternate round, or as specified, to keep the motif flat.

If you are making one large motif, such as a traycloth, it is advisable to change to a circular needle as soon as you have sufficient stitches to reach from one needle point to another. Here again, mark the beginning of the rounds with contrasting yarn.

Casting off must be worked very loosely so as not to distort the edge of the motif. Use a needle one or two sizes larger to cast off in the usual way.

Square motif

This is easier to work with five needles so take one extra needle from a second set of four.

Square motif – increasing by working twice into same stitch

29

Cast on 8 stitches, 2 on each of four needles to form a square.

1st and every alt round K.

2nd round K into front and back of each st – called Kfb. 16 sts.

4th round *Kfb, K2, Kfb, rep from * 3 times more. 24 sts.

6th round *Kfb, K4, Kfb, rep from * 3 times more. 32 sts.

8th round *Kfb, K6, Kfb, rep from * 3 times more. 40 sts.

Continue increasing in this way on every alternate round until the size required. Cast off.

Hexagonal motif

This is worked on four needles. Cast on 6 stitches, 2 on each of three needles to form a triangle.

1st round K.

2nd round *K1, bring the yarn forward between the needles, then over the top of the right-hand needle to increase one – called yfwd –, rep from * 5 times more. 12 sts.

3rd round K.

4th round *K1, yfwd, rep from * 11 times more. 24 sts.

5th and 6th rounds K.

7th round *K1, yfwd, K3, yfwd, rep from * 5 times more. 36 sts.

8th and 9th rounds K.

10th round *K1, yfwd, K5, yfwd, rep from * 5 times more. 48 sts.

11th and 12th rounds K.

13th round *K1, yfwd, K7, yfwd, rep from * 5 times more. 60 sts.

Continue increasing in this way on every following 3rd round until the required size. Cast off.

Circular motif

This requires five needles as given for the square motif. Cast on 8 stitches, 2 on each of four needles to form a square.

1st round K.

2nd round *K1, pick up loop lying between needles and K into back of it – called M1 –, rep from * to end. 16 sts.

Hexagonal motif – increasing worked by taking yarn over right-hand needle to form an eyelet hole

Circular motif – increasing worked by picking up loop lying between stitches.

30

3rd, 4th and 5th rounds K.
6th round As 2nd. 32 sts.
7th, 8th and 9th rounds K.
10th round *K2, M1, rep from * to end. 48 sts.
11th, 12th and 13th rounds K.
14th round *K3, M1, rep from * to end. 64 sts.

15th, 16th and 17th rounds K.
18th round *K4, M1, rep from * to end. 80 sts.
Continue increasing in this way on every following 4th round until the required size. Cast off.

Project for beginners

Knitting and shaping in rounds on four needles.

Pull-on hat

To fit an adult head.
Total quantity of yarn required, 100 g of double knitting.
Set of four 4 mm needles pointed at both ends.

Using set of 4 mm needles cast on a total of 112 stitches: 37 on first needle; 37 on second needle and 38 on third needle. Begin at brim and work in rounds of garter stitch as follows:
1st round P.
2nd round K.
Continue in garter stitch until work measures 10 cm from beginning.
Continue in rounds of stocking stitch (every round K), until work measures 20 cm from beginning.

SHAPE TOP

1st round *K12, K2 tog, rep from * 7 times more. 104 sts.
2nd round K.
3rd round *K11, K2 tog, rep from * 7 times more. 96 sts.
4th round K.

5th round *K10, K2 tog, rep from * 7 times more. 88 sts.
6th round K.
Continue decreasing in this way on next and every alt round, keeping decreased stitches in line, until 16 stitches remain, ending with a plain round.
Next round *K2 tog, rep from * 7 times more. 8 sts.
 Break off yarn leaving an end about 20 cm long. Thread this end into a sewing needle and lift each stitch off the knitting needle and on to the sewing needle. Pull the yarn up tightly to close the top and fasten off securely.
 Fold brim in half to right side. Trim side of brim with 2 pompons (see Chapter 10).

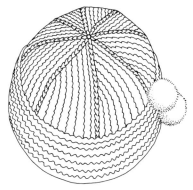

Pull-on hat

5

Coloured knitting

The true appeal of knitting is the infinite variations of fabric which can be achieved by quite simple means. Once you begin to experiment with coloured knitting you will discover how easy it is to work stripes and mosaic patterns to give a new dimension to the craft.

How to work stripes

Any number of colours can be used to produce horizontal, vertical or diagonal stripes, using the methods given here.

Horizontal stripes

This is the simplest way of beginning to experiment with colour and you can adapt any basic stocking stitch design by this means. Two points to remember – each colour must be in the same thickness of yarn and the quantities given in an existing pattern using one colour only will not apply. However, it is a very useful way of using up oddments of yarn.

The stripes can be changed at regular intervals or can be worked over any number of rows, odd or even. If an odd number of rows is worked with one colour you must ensure that the next colour to be used is at the correct edge of the work, otherwise it must be broken off and rejoined.

Each new colour must be joined in at the beginning of a row by inserting the needle into the first stitch and forming the end of the new yarn into a slip loop on the right-hand needle. Pull this loop through to complete the stitch in the usual way. Work the next stitch of the row using both ends of the new yarn to secure it, then continue to the end of the row using the end from the main ball of yarn only.

Unless working an odd number of rows, do not break off the yarn when you have completed each stripe but carry it loosely up the side of the work until it is required again,

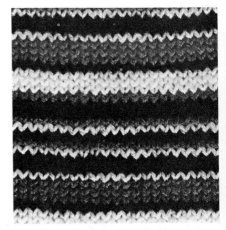

Horizontal stripes showing unbroken line of colour on knitted row

32

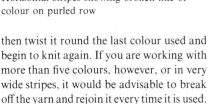

Horizontal stripes showing broken line of colour on purled row

Chevron stripes

then twist it round the last colour used and begin to knit again. If you are working with more than five colours, however, or in very wide stripes, it would be advisable to break off the yarn and rejoin it every time it is used.

If a new colour is brought in on a knitted row every time, the right side of the fabric will show an unbroken line of colour and the purl side will show a broken line of colour. Stripes can be worked in the same way over ribbing but if you want to keep an unbroken line of colour on the right side of the fabric, the first row of each new change of colour on the right side must be knitted throughout.

Chevron stripes

This beautiful, undulating pattern is achieved by working in horizontal stripes and the chevron effect is formed by increasing and decreasing at certain points in the same row. It cannot be worked over any number of stitches as it requires set multiples of stitches to ensure that the pattern works out correctly but the width of each

chevron can be varied by knitting more, or less stitches between the shaping. The pattern given here is worked over multiples of thirteen stitches, plus two edge stitches.

1st row (RS) *K2, increase one by picking up loop between needles and knitting into the back – called inc 1 –, K4, slip the next stitch from the left-hand needle to the right-hand needle in a knit-wise direction – called sl 1 K-wise –, K2 together, pass the slipped stitch over the K2 together – called psso –, K4, inc 1, repeat from * to last 2 stitches, K2.

2nd row P.

These 2 rows form the pattern and the colours can be changed as required.

Vertical stripes

This method is more difficult to work as the colours are changed several times in the same row. When working narrow stripes of not more than four or five stitches, the yarn not in use is carried very loosely across the back of the work until it is required again,

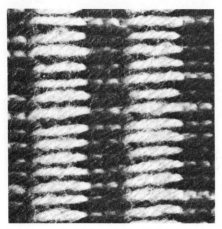

Narrow vertical stripes, back of fabric, showing correct stranding

Narrow vertical stripes, back of fabric, showing incorrect stranding

then simply continue knitting with the new colour and drop the last colour. This method gives a fabric of double thickness; it is important to strand the yarn loosely across the back of the work to avoid a puckered appearance.

When working wider stripes, each colour must be knitted with a separate ball of yarn. In the example shown here two colours have been used and, as is usual with coloured knitting, the first colour used has been coded as A and the second as B. The fabric begins with a stripe in A and ends with a stripe in B.

1st row (R S) *Knit the required number of stitches with A, then hold A to the left at the back of the work. Pick up B and carry it to the right at the back of the work, under and over the strand of A. Using B knit the required number of stitches. Then change

Changing colours on a knit row

colours again by holding B to the left, pick up A and carry it to the right at the back of the work under and over the strand of B. Repeat from * to the end of the row, ending with B.

Wide vertical stripes using separate balls of yarn

34

2nd row *Purl the required number of stitches with B, then hold B to the left at the front of the work. Pick up A and carry it to the right at the front of the work under

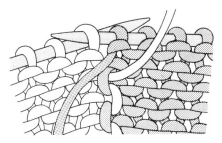

Changing colours on a purl row

Narrow diagonal stripes

and over the strand of B. Using A purl the required number of stitches, then hold A to the left at the front of the work and pick up B. Carry it to the right at the front of the work under and over the strand of A. Repeat from * to the end of the row, ending with A.

These 2 rows form the pattern.

Diagonal stripes

The same method is used to achieve diagonal stripes as explained for vertical stripes. The slant is obtained by working one or more stitches to the right or left on every row, or alternate rows, depending on the diagonal angle required.

The example shown here uses two colours, again coded as A and B, and requires multiples of 4 stitches plus 2 edge stitches.

1st row (RS) K2 with A, *K2 with B, K2 with A, rep from * to end.
2nd row Pl with B, *P2 with A, P2 with B, rep from * to last stitch, Pl with A.
3rd row K2 with B, *K2 with A, K2 with B, rep from * to end.

4th row Pl with A, *P2 with B, P2 with A, rep from * to last stitch, Pl with B.

These 4 rows form the pattern.

Mosaic patterns

These patterns may appear quite complicated but they are achieved by working in horizontal stripes and slipping stitches without working them at certain intervals. The slipped stitches give a broken appearance to the stripes and produce a most attractive fabric.

The two examples given here are both worked over the same multiples of stitches so you can alternate them, or combine them with bands of plain stripes to produce an allover fabric.

Turret stitch

The colours used are coded as A and B and the stitch is worked over multiples of 4 stitches plus 3 edge stitches.
1st row (RS) Using A, K.
2nd row Using A, P.

35

Turret stitch

Alternating turret stitch

3rd row Using B, K3, *keeping yarn at back slip the next stitch from left-hand needle to right-hand needle in a purl-wise direction – called sl 1 –, K3, rep from * to end.
4th row Using B, K3, *bring yarn forward between needles and sl 1, take yarn back between needles and K3, rep from * to end.
5th row Using A, K2, *keeping yarn at back sl 1, K1, rep from * to last st, K1.
6th row Using A, P2, *keeping yarn at front sl 1, P1, rep from * to last st, P1.
7th row Using B, K1, *keeping yarn at back sl 1, K3, rep from * to last 2 sts, keeping yarn at back sl 1, K1.
8th row Using B, K1, *bring yarn forward between needles and sl 1, take yarn back and K3, rep from * to last 2 sts, bring yarn forward and sl 1, take yarn back and K1.
9th and 10th rows As 1st and 2nd.
11th and 12th rows As 7th and 8th.
13th and 14th rows As 5th and 6th.
15th and 16th rows As 3rd and 4th.
These 16 rows form the pattern.

Alternating turret stitch

Work first 4 rows as given for turret stitch.
5th row Using A, K1, *keeping yarn at back sl 1, K3, rep from * to last 2 sts, sl 1, K1.
6th row Using A, K1, *bring yarn forward and sl 1, take yarn back and K3, rep from * to last 2 sts, bring yarn forward and sl 1, take yarn back and K1.
7th row Using B, K2, *keeping yarn at back sl 1, K1, rep from * to last st, K1.
8th row Using B, K2, *bring yarn forward and sl 1, take yarn back and K1, rep from * to last st, K1.
9th and 10th rows Using A, as 3rd and 4th.
11th and 12th rows Using B, as 5th and 6th.
13th and 14th rows Using A, as 1st and 2nd.
15th and 16th rows As 11th and 12th.
17th and 18th rows As 9th and 10th.
19th and 20th rows As 7th and 8th.
21st and 22nd rows As 5th and 6th.
23rd and 24th rows As 3rd and 4th.
These 24 rows form the pattern.

Project for beginners

Combining stripes and mosaic stitches.

Woman's jersey

To fit 86 cm bust.
Total quantity of yarn required, 650 g of double knitting.

Back

Using 4 mm needles – or the correct size to give a tension of 24 sts and 32 rows to 10 cm over stocking stitch (see Chapter 3), cast on 111 sts. Using colours as required work 2 cm garter st; 10 cm horizontal stripes; 2 cm garter st; 10 cm turret st; 2 cm garter st; 10 cm horizontal stripes; 2 cm garter st; 10 cm alternating turret st; 2 cm garter st;

10 cm horizontal stripes and 2 cm garter st. Cast off loosely.

Front

Work as given for back.

Sleeves

Using 4 mm needles or size required, work in same colours as for back and cast on 99 sts. Work 10 cm garter st for turned-back cuff. Work 10 cm horizontal stripes; 2 cm garter st; 10 cm turret st; 2 cm garter st; 10 cm horizontal stripes and 2 cm garter st. Cast off loosely.

Do not press. Join pieces as shown in diagram.

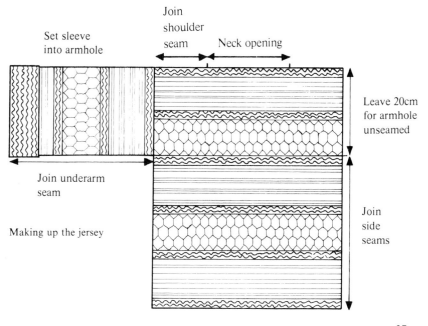

Set sleeve into armhole

Join shoulder seam

Neck opening

Leave 20cm for armhole unseamed

Join underarm seam

Making up the jersey

Join side seams

37

Fair Isle and Jacquard

To continue exploring the full possibilities of coloured knitting, you now need to experiment with the techniques for working Shetland, Fair Isle, collage and jacquard patterns.

The first two methods use any two colours at one time in the same row, stranding or weaving the yarn not in use across the back of the work to produce a fabric of double thickness.

The last two methods can bring an unlimited number of colours into use in the same row; small, separate balls of each colour are required, as given for wide vertical stripes in Chapter 5, to give a fabric of single thickness.

Shetland and Fair Isle patterns

These types of patterns are sometimes confused but, as a general rule, Shetland patterns produce an all-over fabric, whereas Fair Isle patterns are used as bands of coloured knitting. The working methods are the same for both techniques.

Shetland and Fair Isle charts

These designs are usually set out in chart form on graph paper, with one square representing one stitch and one row of squares denoting a complete row. Each colour is given a different code, such as A, B, C and so on, and these are represented by different symbols on the chart. The first and every following odd numbered row on the chart is worked from right to left for flat knitting, and the second and following even numbered rows are purled from left to right. When working in rounds, the right side of the fabric is always facing you so each round is worked from right to left.

To ensure that the patterns work out exactly, use a multiple of the number of stitches needed for each repeat; additional edge stitches, which are not repeated, will be given at the beginnings or endings of each row.

Working Shetland and Fair Isle patterns

Stocking stitch is used to produce these patterns and one colour is used to form the background, with the second colour producing the pattern. When a colour is not in use it is carried across the back of the fabric until it is required again, using either the 'stranding' or 'weaving' method.

Both of these methods are explained in detail on p. 44. You should experiment with each of them to ensure that you can produce a neat and even fabric.

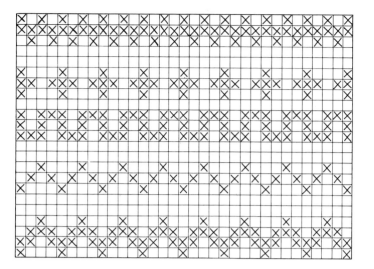

☐ = A

☒ = B

Repeats of
4 sts +1

Fair Isle patterns

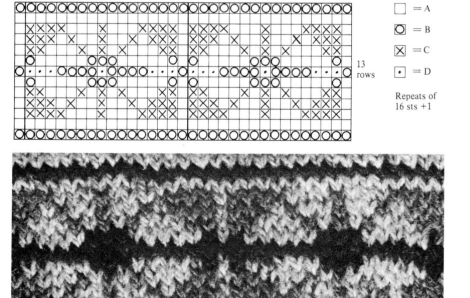

☐ = A

Ⓞ = B

☒ = C

• = D

13
rows

Repeats of
16 sts +1

Small Fair Isle patterns

39

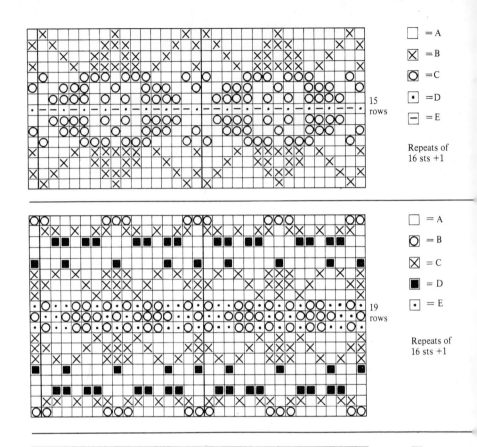

□ = A
☒ = B
◎ = C
• = D
— = E

15 rows

Repeats of
16 sts +1

□ = A
◎ = B
☒ = C
■ = D
• = E

19 rows

Repeats of
16 sts +1

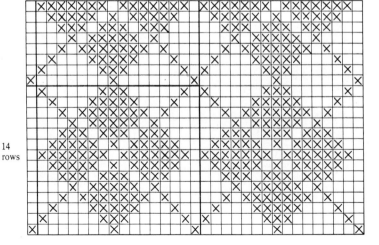

□ = A
☒ = B

Repeats of
16 sts +1

14 rows

Fair Isle patterns

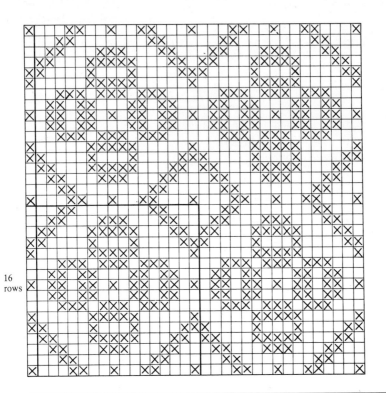

☐ = A

☒ = B

Repeats of 16 sts +1

16 rows

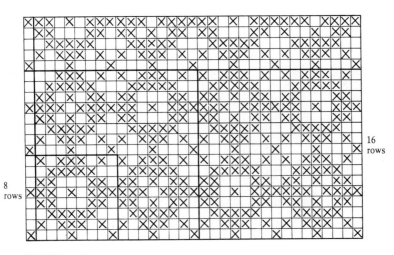

☐ = A

☒ = B

Repeats of 16 sts +1
OR
Repeats of 8 sts +1

16 rows

8 rows

Fair Isle patterns

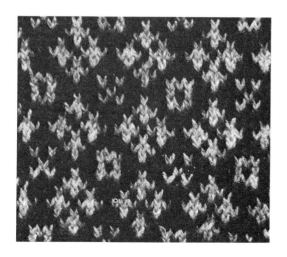

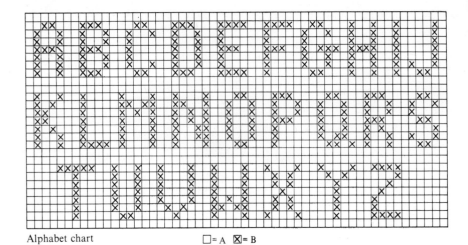

Alphabet chart   □ = A   ⊠ = B

Stranding yarns

Use the first colour to knit the required number of stitches, then take the second colour across the back of the work very loosely and knit the required number of stitches with this colour. On a purl row the colour not in use is carried across the front of the work and when working in rounds it is always carried across the back of the work.

You will find it easier to work with two balls of yarn if the colour in use is held in the right hand and the colour not in use held in the left hand, to avoid the balls becoming too entangled.

Stranding may be used where not more than four or five stitches are being worked in one colour.

Weaving yarns

If more than five stitches are worked in any colour, stranding the yarn across the back results in very untidy threads which can easily catch and break. It is much neater to weave the yarn not in use in with every

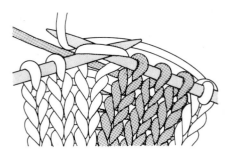

Stranding yarn across back

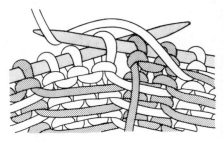

Stranding yarn across front

44

second or third stitch being knitted with the first colour.

Hold the two balls of yarn as given for stranding and knit the first stitch; then on

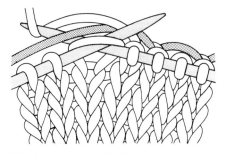

Weaving yarn across back

the second and every following second or third stitch, put the point of the right-hand needle into the stitch, carry the yarn in the left hand over the top of the right-hand needle and knit the stitch with the yarn in the right hand in the usual way. This catches the second colour in place without it showing on the right side of the fabric.

On a purl row the yarn is woven across the front of the work in the same way but weaving it in on the first and every following second or third stitch.

Collage and jacquard patterns

Collage patterns can be used to produce areas of different colours, usually completely irregular, as with patchwork effects, or as a complete scene creating an art form in yarn. This method uses small balls of yarn for each section, as given for vertical stripes in Chapter 5.

Sometimes it is also necessary to weave or strand one of the colours across a few

stitches to make sure that it is in the right place for working the next row.

When using a lot of colours they are easier to handle if each small ball is wound round a bobbin, to hang at the back of the work and help keep the yarn free of tangles.

Jacquard patterns are normally used to create a single, multicoloured motif or bands of pattern which use more than two colours in the same row.

The technique for these patterns can use all three methods of stranding, weaving or separate balls of yarn, depending on the area of each colour being worked.

Patchwork patterns

This form of collage knitting produces a most attractive fabric. The permutations in arranging the patches and colours are almost endless and you can also combine them with bands of horizontal or vertical stripes to give even more scope.

A beginner will find it easier to knit the patches in strips and then join them together but a more advanced knitter will be able to assess the overall width of the fabric required and then knit each patch in sequence across the total number of stitches.

The examples given here have all been colour coded, the first colour used as A, the second as B, the third as C, and so on. They have all been worked over 24 stitches and 32 rows to complete each patch, using a 4 mm needle or the size required to give a patch 10 cm square, using double knitting yarn.

First patch

Using A, cast on 24 sts.
1st row (RS) Using A, K to end.
2nd row Using B, P1, using A, P23.
3rd row Using A, K22, using B, K2.

Second patch

First patch

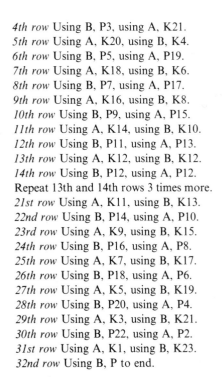

4th row Using B, P3, using A, K21.
5th row Using A, K20, using B, K4.
6th row Using B, P5, using A, P19.
7th row Using A, K18, using B, K6.
8th row Using B, P7, using A, P17.
9th row Using A, K16, using B, K8.
10th row Using B, P9, using A, P15.
11th row Using A, K14, using B, K10.
12th row Using B, P11, using A, P13.
13th row Using A, K12, using B, K12.
14th row Using B, P12, using A, P12.
Repeat 13th and 14th rows 3 times more.
21st row Using A, K11, using B, K13.
22nd row Using B, P14, using A, P10.
23rd row Using A, K9, using B, K15.
24th row Using B, P16, using A, P8.
25th row Using A, K7, using B, K17.
26th row Using B, P18, using A, P6.
27th row Using A, K5, using B, K19.
28th row Using B, P20, using A, P4.
29th row Using A, K3, using B, K21.
30th row Using B, P22, using A, P2.
31st row Using A, K1, using B, K23.
32nd row Using B, P to end.

Second patch

Using C, work 4 rows st st.
5th row Using C, K8, using D, K8, using C, K8.
6th row Using C, P7, using D, P10, using C, P7.
7th row Using C, K6, using D, K12, using C, K6.
8th row Using C, P5, using D, P14, using C, P5.
9th row Using C, K4, using D, K16, using C, K4.
10th row Using C, P3, using D, P18, using C, P3.
11th row Using C, K3, using D, K18, using C, K3.
Repeat 10th and 11th rows 6 times more.
24th row P as 9th.
25th row K as 8th.
26th row P as 7th.
27th row K as 6th.
28th row P as 5th.
Using C, work 4 rows st st.

Third patch

Fourth patch

Third patch

1st row Using E, K8, using F, K8, using G, K8.

2nd row Using G, P7, using F, P8, using E, P8, using G, P1.

3rd row Using G, K2, using E, K8, using F, K8, using G, K6.

4th row Using G, P5, using F, P8, using E, P8, using G, P3.

Continue in this way moving one st to the left on every K row and one st to the right on every P row, until 32 rows have been completed, bringing in each colour in turn.

Fourth patch

1st row Using H, K24.

2nd row Using I, P1, using H, P22, using J, P1.

3rd row Using J, K2, using H, K20, using I, K2.

4th row Using I, P3, using H, P18, using J, P3.

5th row Using J, K4, using H, K16, using I, K4.

6th row Using I, P5, using H, P14, using J, P5.

7th row Using J, K6, using H, K12, using I, K6.

8th row Using I, P7, using H, P10, using J, P7.

9th row Using J, K8, using H, K8, using I, K8.

10th row Using I, P9, using H, P6, using J, P9.

11th row Using J, K10, using H, K4, using I, K10.

12th row Using I, P11, using H, P2, using J, P11.

13th row Using J, K12, using I, K12.

14th row Using I, P12, using J, P12.

Repeat 13th and 14th rows 3 times more.

21st row K as 12th, reading K for H, to end of patch.

22nd row P as 11th.

23rd row K as 10th.

24th row P as 9th.

25th row K as 8th.

26th row P as 7th.
27th row K as 6th.
28th row P as 5th.
29th row K as 4th.
30th row P as 3rd.
31st row K as 2nd.
32nd row Using K, P to end.

Jacquard motif

A multicoloured motif can be used to high-light a basic jersey on the bodice, sleeves, or as a patch pocket. Each colour has been coded on the chart given here.

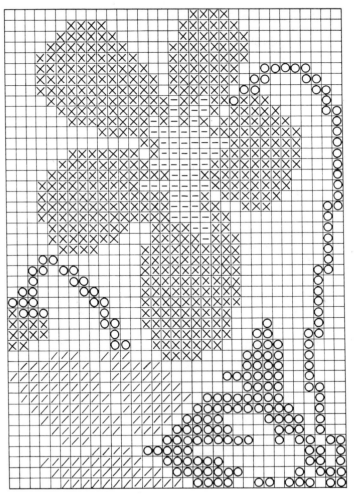

☐ = A. Cream

☒ = B. Violet

Ⓞ = C. Green

⊟ = D. Yellow

⧄ = E. Light green

Jacquard motif

Project for advanced knitters

Combining patchwork patterns to form an overall fabric. (Beginners can also work this design in strips.)

Cushion cover

To fit 40 cm cushion pad.
Total quantity of yarn required, 250 g of double knitting.

Cushion front

Using 4 mm needles, or size required to obtain 24 sts and 32 rows to 10 cm, cast on a total of 96 sts, 24 for first patch, 24 for second patch, 24 for third patch and 24 for fourth patch. Work 32 rows in pattern. Cont in pattern, alternating patches as given in diagram, until 4 complete patches have been worked. Cast off.

Work back in same way, or using A only work in st st.

With RS of both pieces facing, join 3 edges. Turn to RS. Insert pad. Join remaining seam, inserting zip fastener if required.

1st	2nd	4th	3rd
3rd	4th	1st	2nd
1st	2nd	3rd	4th
4th	3rd	2nd	1st

Cushion cover

7

Travelling patterns

Knitted fabrics are not just formed by inter-locking one stitch into the same stitch of the previous row or round. The apparent rigidity of knitting can become beautifully fluid, or light and lacy in texture, by moving the position of certain stitches in a row, or by extending the length of the stitches.

Moving the direction of stitches

This method can be used to form simple twisted effects, zig-zag and diamond patterns criss-crossing the surface of the fabric, or plaited and interlaced ropes or cables.

Some of the simpler effects can be achieved by working the stitches in the row out of sequence but the more complex structure of cable stitches needs a separate cable needle to hold the stitches until they are ready to be worked.

Twisted stitches

The same two or three stitches can be twisted to the right or left on every right-side row to form vertical lines which stand out in relief against the fabric. The twisted stitches should be knitted and show to best effect if they are worked on a reversed stocking stitch background.

Twisting stitches to the right

To twist two stitches, knit into the front of the second stitch on the left-hand needle, then into the front of the first stitch and slip both stitches off the needle together. The abbreviation for this is Tw2R.

To twist three stitches, knit into the front of the third stitch on the left-hand needle, then into the front of the second and first

Twisting two stitches to the right

Twisting three stitches to the right

Twisting three stitches to the left

stitches, and slip all three stitches off the needle together. The abbreviation for this is Tw3R.

Twisting stitches to the left

To twist two stitches, knit into the back of the second stitch on the left-hand needle, then into the front of the first stitch and slip

Twisting two stitches to the left

both stitches off the needle together. The abbreviation for this is Tw2L.

To twist three stitches, knit into the back of the third stitch on the left-hand needle, then into the back of the second stitch and front of the first stitch, and slip all three stitches off the needle together. The abbreviation for this is Tw3L.

Zig-zag stitches

Combining twisted stitches to the right and left can be used to form ridged surface patterns of almost any shape.

Diamond panel

The sample shown here has been worked as a panel over a total of 20 stitches, with the diamond shape twisted against a knitted background.

1st row (R S) K8, Tw2R, Tw2L, K8.
2nd and every alt row P to end.
3rd row K7, Tw2R, K2, Tw2L, K7.
5th row K6, Tw2R, K4, Tw2L, K6.
7th row K5, Tw2R, K6, Tw2L, K5.

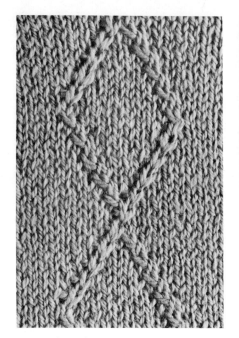

Diamond panel

Twisted braid

9th row K4, Tw2R, K8, Tw2L, K4.
11th row K4, Tw2L, K8, Tw2R, K4.
13th row K5, Tw2L, K6, Tw2R, K5.
15th row K6, Tw2L, K4, Tw2R, K6.
17th row K7, Tw2L, K2, Tw2R, K7.
19th row K8, Tw2L, Tw2R, K8.
21st row K9, Tw2R, K9.
22nd row P to end.
These 22 rows form the pattern.

Twisted braid

This simple pattern requires 10 stitches for each panel.
1st row (WS) K3, P5, K2.
2nd row P2, K3, Tw2R, P3.
3rd row As 1st.
4th row P2, Tw2L, Tw2R, Tw2L, P2.
5th row K2, P5, K3.
6th row P3, Tw2L, K3, P2.
7th row As 5th.

8th row P2, Tw2R, Tw2L, Tw2R, P2.
These 8 rows form the pattern.

Cable patterns

A separate cable needle as well as a pair of needles is required to work these stitches. The cable needle is short and double-pointed and should be of the same thickness as the needles used for the main fabric.

The rope-like twists of cables can be moved to the left or right and combined in many ways over large multiples of stitches.

Cable twist to the right

The sample shown here uses six stitches for the cable, which is knitted against a purl background over a total of twenty stitches.

Cable twist to the right

A cable can be worked over different even numbers, such as four or eight; the abbreviation – C4, C8 and so on – will include the total figure over which the cable is worked.

1st row (R S) P7, K6, P7.
2nd row K7, P6, K7.
Repeat these 2 rows twice more.
7th row P7, slip next 3 stitches on to a cable needle and hold at the back of the work, knit the next 3 stitches from the left-hand needle, then knit the 3 stitches from the cable needle – abbreviated as C6B –, P7.
8th row As 2nd.
These 8 rows form the pattern.

Cable twist to the left

For this sample, cast on and work the first 6 rows as given for cable twist to the right.
7th row P7, slip next 3 stitches on to a cable needle and hold at the front of the work, knit the next 3 stitches from the left-hand needle, then knit the 3 stitches from the

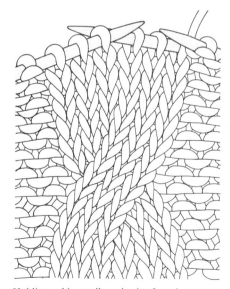

Holding cable needle at back of work

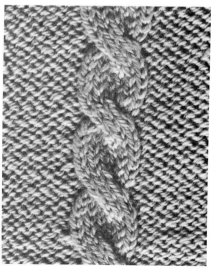

Cable twist to the left

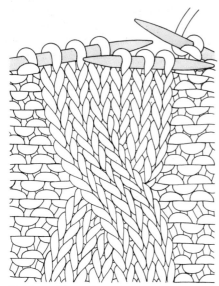

Braided cable

This effective cable uses twists to the right and left. The sample shown here uses eight stitches for the cables, which are knitted against a purl background, over a total of twenty stitches.

1st row (WS) K6, P8, K6.
2nd row P6, (C4B) twice, P6.
3rd row As 1st.
4th row P6, K8, P6.
5th row As 1st.
6th row P6, (C4F) twice, P6.
7th row As 1st.
8th row As 4th.
These 8 rows form the pattern.

Holding cable needle at front of work

Crossed cable

cable needle – abbreviated as C6F –, P7.
8th row As 2nd.
These 8 rows form the pattern.

The sample shown here uses six stitches for the cable, which is knitted against a purl background, over a total of ten stitches.

Braided cable

1st row (RS) P2, K6, P2.
2nd row K2, P6, K2.
Repeat these 2 rows twice more.
7th row P2, C6B, P2.
8th row As 2nd.
Repeat 1st and 2nd rows twice more.
13th row P4, K2, P4.
14th row K4, P2, K4.
Repeat 13th and 14th rows 3 times more
These 20 rows form the pattern.

Lengthening stitches

These stitches cannot be classed as authentic lace patterns but they are very simple to work and give an openwork effect. This method lengthens the stitches by winding the yarn round the right-hand needle more than once before completing the stitch.

Elongated garter stitch

Any number of stitches can be used to form this pattern and every row is knitted so the fabric is reversible.

1st row K1, *K next st winding the yarn 3 times round the right-hand needle before completing the st, repeat from * to last st, K1.
2nd row K1, *K next st dropping extra loops off left-hand needle, repeat from * to the last st, K1.
These 2 rows form the pattern.

Elongated lace stitch

This pattern requires multiples of 3 stitches plus 2 edge stitches and is worked throughout in garter stitch.
1st row (RS) K1, *K next st winding yarn 3 times round right-hand needle before completing the st, repeat from * to the last st, K1.
2nd row K1, *slip next 3 sts off the left-hand needle on to the right-hand needle dropping the extra loops, place these 3 sts back on to

Elongated garter stitch

Elongated lace stitch

55

left-hand needle and knit them together through the back of the loops, repeat from * to the last st, K1.

3rd row K1, *K into front, back and front of next st to make 3 sts, repeat from * to the last st, K1.

4th row K to end.

These 4 rows form the pattern.

Project for beginners

Working elongated stitches.

Evening stole

40 cm wide by 152 cm long, excluding fringe. Total quantity of yarn required, 200 g of mohair.

Using a pair of 7 mm needles, or size required to give correct width, cast on 62 sts by the thumb method.

Work in elongated garter stitch or elongated lace pattern until work measures 152 cm from beginning. Cast off very loosely.

Cut yarn into 40 cm lengths. Take 2 strands at a time and knot fringe into every alternate stitch along cast on and cast off edges (see Chapter 10).

Evening stole in mohair

Guernsey and Aran patterns

Traditional fishermen's Guernseys are based on simple textured stitches, such as moss stitch and travelling stitches, to achieve twisted and cabled patterns. The original Guernseys were worked in a very thick yarn on exceptionally fine needles, to give a wind and weatherproof fabric with the appearance of a closely woven brocade. They required very little shaping and would be worked in rounds on sets of five double-pointed needles to form a completely seamless garment.

The knitting of the Aran Isles, which lie off the west coast of Ireland, is instantly recognizable by its richly encrusted texture. With the exception of the introduction of 'bobble' stitches, the patterns used are based on Guernsey stitches but the softer Aran or bainin yarn is worked on thicker needles and the entire area of the fabric is criss-crossed to give an almost three-dimensional effect. The shape also differs from an authentic fisherman's Guernsey, with the back, front and sleeves being worked separately and seamed together afterwards.

The real skill in both versions was the way in which the stitches were grouped together and the many variations on basic techniques which were devised by the knitters. Each coastal area of Britain developed its own regional patterns and any fisherman could tell at a glance where another came from, purely from the arrangement of stitches on his 'gansey'.

Panels of both Guernsey and Aran stitches have been given in this chapter and you can use these singly to highlight an otherwise plain garment, or begin to experiment by combining them to form an all-over fabric.

Guernsey patterns

These stitches were originally based on very simple, everyday objects and events and they are still referred to by their traditional names.

Diamond or net stitch

The diamond is worked in Irish moss stitch against a stocking stitch background and requires 13 stitches to complete, but any number of stitches can be worked on either side. The sample shown here has been worked as a panel of 15 stitches.
1st row (R S) K.
2nd row P.
3rd row K7, P1, K7.
4th row P7, K1, P7.
5th row K6, P1, K1, P1, K6.
6th row P6, K1, P1, K1, P6.
7th row K5, (P1, K1) twice, P1, K5.
8th row P5, (K1, P1) twice, K1, P5.
9th row K4, (P1, K1) 3 times, P1, K4.
10th row P4, (K1, P1) 3 times, K1, P4.
11th row K3, (P1, K1) 4 times, P1, K3.
12th row P3, (K1, P1) 4 times, K1, P3.

Diamond or net stitch

13th row K2, (P1, K1) 5 times, P1, K2.
14th row P2, (K1, P1) 5 times, K1, P2.
15th row K1, (P1, K1) 6 times, P1, K1.
16th row P1, (K1, P1) 6 times, K1, P1.
17th and 18th rows As 13th and 14th.
19th and 20th rows As 11th and 12th.
21st and 22nd rows As 9th and 10th.
23rd and 24th rows As 7th and 8th.
25th and 26th rows As 5th and 6th.

27th and 28th rows As 3rd and 4th.
These 28 rows form the pattern.

Ladder stitch

This simple stitch can be worked over any number of stitches and is useful as a linking panel between more complicated patterns.
1st row (RS) K.
2nd row P.
Rep these 2 rows once more, then 1st row once more.
6th row K.
These 6 rows form the pattern.

Herringbone stitch

The sample shown here has been worked as a panel of 15 stitches.
1st row (RS) K7, P1, K7.
2nd row P6, K1, P1, K1, P6.
3rd row K5, P1, K3, P1, K5.
4th row P4, K1, P5, K1, P4.
5th row K3, P1, K7, P1, K3.
6th row P2, K1, P9, K1, P2.
These 6 rows form the pattern.

Ladder stitch

Herringbone stitch

Marriage lines

This traditional stitch portrays the ups and downs of married life! The sample shown here has been worked as a panel of 15 stitches.

1st row (RS) K9, P1, K2, P1, K2.
2nd row P1, K1, P2, K1, P10.
3rd row As 1st.
4th row P3, K1, P2, K1, P8.
5th row K7, P1, K2, P1, K4.
6th row P5, K1, P2, K1, P6.
7th row K5, P1, K2, P1, K6.
8th row P7, K1, P2, K1, P4.
9th row K3, P1, K2, P1, K8.
10th row P9, K1, P2, K1, P2.
11th row K1, P1, K2, P1, K10.
12th row As 10th.
13th row As 9th.
14th row As 8th.
15th row As 7th.
16th row As 6th.
17th row As 5th.
18th row As 4th.
These 18 rows form the pattern.

Marriage lines

Irish moss stitch

Aran patterns

Many of these stitches gained religious significance and were adapted from the Irish stones and crosses, using intricate interlaced and plaited cables. The bobble stitch also plays an important part in the formation of richly decorated fabrics which are renowned throughout the knitting world.

Irish moss stitch

This forms an ideal linking pattern between panels, particularly at the side edges where shaping may be required.

Beginning the first row with a knitted stitch, work 2 rows as given for single rib (see Chapter 2). Beginning the 3rd row with a purled stitch work 2 more rows single rib. These 4 rows form the pattern.

Trinity stitch

This small bobble stitch has a religious background, as its name implies, derived from

Trinity stitch

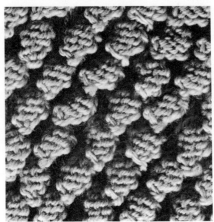

Bobble stitch

the working method of '3 into 1 and 1 into 3'. This stitch requires multiples of 4 stitches.
1st row (RS) P.
2nd row *P3 tog, (K1, P1, K1) all into next st, rep from * to end.
3rd row P.
4th row *(K1, P1, K1) all into next st, P3 tog, rep from * to end.
These 4 rows form the pattern.

Bobble stitch

The position of each bobble can be varied by working 2 more stitches and rows between each bobble. The sample shown here requires multiples of 4 stitches plus 3 edge stitches.
1st row (RS) K.
2nd row P.
3rd row K3, *(K into front then into back of next st twice, then K into front of same st) making 5 sts, (turn and K5, turn and P5) twice, with left-hand needle lift the 2nd, 3rd, 4th and 5th sts over the first st and off needle – called Bl –, K3, rep from * to end.
4th row P.
Repeat 1st and 2nd rows once more.

7th row K1, *B1, K3, rep from * to last 2 sts, B1, K1.
8th row P.
These 8 rows form the pattern.

Aran diamond and bobble stitch

The sample shown here has been worked as a panel of 15 stitches.
1st row (RS) P5, sl next 3 sts on to cable needle and hold at back of work, K2 from left-hand needle, sl the P st on cable needle back on to left-hand needle and P1, K2 from cable needle, P5.
2nd row K5, P2, K1, P2, K5.
3rd row P4, sl next st on to cable needle and hold at back of work, K2 from left-hand needle then P1 from cable needle – called Cb –, K1, sl next 2 sts on to cable needle and hold at front of work, P1 from left-hand needle then K2 from cable needle – called Cf –, P4.
4th and every foll alt row K all P sts and P all K sts of previous row.
5th row P3, Cb, K1, P1, K1, Cf, P3.

7th row P2, Cb, (K1, P1) twice, K1, Cf, P2.
9th row P1, Cb, (K1, P1) 3 times, K1, Cf, P1.
11th row P1, Cf, (P1, K1) 3 times, P1, Cb, P1.
13th row P2, Cf, (P1, K1) twice, P1, Cb, P2.
15th row P3, Cf, P1, K1, P1, Cb, P3.
17th row P4, Cf, P1, Cb, P4.
19th row As 1st.
21st row P4, Cb, P1, Cf, P4.
23rd row P3, Cb, P3, Cf, P3.
25th row P3, K2, P2, B1 (see above), P2, K2, P3.
27th row P3, Cf, P3, Cb, P3.
29th row As 17th.
30th row As 4th.
These 30 rows form the pattern.

Lobster claw stitch

This stitch requires multiples of 9 stitches plus 2 edge stitches and could be worked as a single panel of 11 stitches or as an all-over pattern.

The sample shown here has been worked over 29 stitches.

1st row (RS) P2, *K7, P2, rep from * to end.

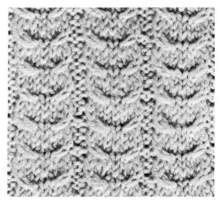

Aran diamond and bobble stitch   Lobster claw stitch

2nd row K2, *P7, K2, rep from * to end.
3rd row P2, *sl next 2 sts on to cable needle and hold at back of work, K1 from left-hand needle, then K2 from cable needle, K1 from left-hand needle, sl next st on to cable needle and hold at front of work, K2 from left-hand needle, then K1 from cable needle, P2, rep from * to end.
4th row As 2nd.
These 4 rows form the pattern.

Project for advanced knitters

Working and combining panels of Aran stitches.

Poncho

To fit an average woman's size.
Length at centre front, approx 63 cm.
Total quantity of yarn required, 750 g of Aran knitting.
One pair 4½ mm needles, one cable needle and one No. 4·00 crochet hook are required.

Using 4½ mm needles cast on 89 sts.
1st row (R S) P2, *K7, P7, K2, P1, K2, P7, rep from * twice more, K7, P2.

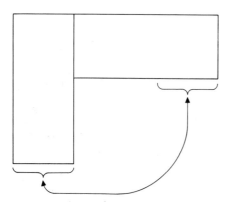

Making up the poncho

2nd row K2, *P7, K7, P2, K1, P2, K7, rep from * twice more, P7, K2.
3rd row P2, *patt 9 sts as 3rd row of lobster claw st, patt 15 sts as 1st row of diamond and bobble st, P2, rep from * twice more, patt 9 sts as 3rd row of lobster claw st.
4th row K2, *patt 9 sts as 4th row of lobster claw st, patt 15 sts as 2nd row of diamond and bobble st, K2, rep from * twice more, patt 9 sts as 4th row of lobster claw st.
5th row P2, *patt 9 sts as 1st row of lobster claw st, patt 15 sts as 21st row of diamond and bobble st, P2, rep from * twice more, patt 9 sts as 1st row of lobster claw st.
6th row K2, *patt 9 sts as 2nd row of lobster claw st, patt 15 sts as 22nd row of diamond and bobble st, K2, rep from * twice more, patt 9 sts as 2nd row of lobster claw st.

Cont in this way, working rep of 4 patt rows for lobster claw st and working rows 23–30 of diamond and bobble st, then rep rows 1–30 of this st 7 times more, then rep 1st and 2nd rows of this st. 226 rows in all. Cast off.

Work a second piece in same way.

Do not press. Join pieces as shown in diagram. Using No. 4·00 crochet hook work 2 rounds of dc round neck and outer edges (see Chapter 10).

The basis of designing

Once you can knit, the step to adapting an existing pattern is very simple. All you need to know are the exact measurements of the garment you have in mind and the exact tension, from an existing set of instructions. To begin designing for yourself you need exact measurements and you need to know the number of stitches and rows you obtain to 10 centimetres with the yarn and needle size of your choice.

If you are a beginner it is best to make your first attempt at adapting a pattern as simple as possible, using a double knitting quality which can be worked on 4 mm needles to give a firm fabric, and a basic set of instructions in stocking stitch – this will give you the tension you require. Then begin to experiment by working in one of the simple stitches or techniques given in the previous chapters – random horizontal stripes would be ideal and would give a completely different appearance to the finished garment.

If you wish to begin designing for yourself you are no longer restricted to working from a given tension. Work a tension sample in the yarn you want to use, making sure that the needle size is not too fine so that the fabric feels thick and felted, or too large so that the fabric feels limp. Measure the sample to see how many stitches and rows you have obtained to 10 centimetres (see Chapter 3), which will give you the basis for all your calculations.

Body measurements

Whether you wish to adapt a pattern to fit a smaller or larger size, or design a garment for yourself, you need to know your own exact measurements. The width and length of each piece of the garment must then be calculated, based on the tension you are using. An extra number of stitches and rows must then be added to this total to allow for what is referred to as 'tolerance'. This ensures ease of movement – an overall width tolerance of approximately 5 centimetres is sufficient for most garments. Obviously, a thick chunky jacket which is intended to be worn over another garment will require more tolerance than a slim-fitting T shirt. This amount will already have been included in an existing set of instructions.

Amending existing pattern sizes

This must be based on the stitch and row tension given in the instructions, say, 24 stitches and 32 rows to 10 centimetres worked on 4 mm needles as an example. By placing a decimal point between the number of stitches given for 10 centimetres, you can arrive at the number of stitches needed for each centimetre, e.g. in this case there are 2·4 stitches to 1 centimetre.

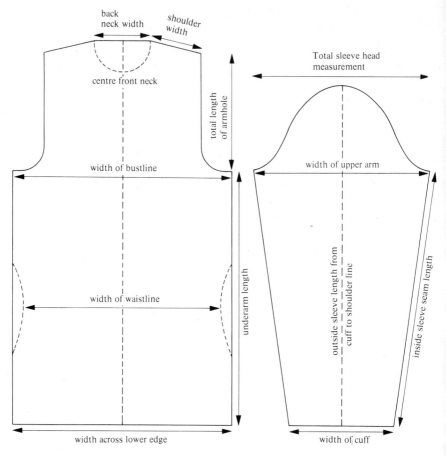

back neck width
shoulder width

centre front neck

total length of armhole

Total sleeve head measurement

width of bustline

width of upper arm

width of waistline

underarm length

outside sleeve length from cuff to shoulder line

inside sleeve seam length

width across lower edge

width of cuff

Measurements required for basic jersey body   Measurements required for basic jersey sleeve

Based on this example the width and length of a basic jersey can be adjusted up or down by adding or subtracting 2·4 stitches and 3·2 rows for every centimetre difference in width and length required, adjusting these figures to the nearest whole number. You must remember to make provision for this difference in the original total given when any shaping is required, allowing approximately a third of the difference for the underarm shaping, a third for the shoulders and the remaining third for the neck.

Designing for yourself

Once you have selected the yarn, needle size and stitch which will give you the fabric you require, you need to plan the shape of the

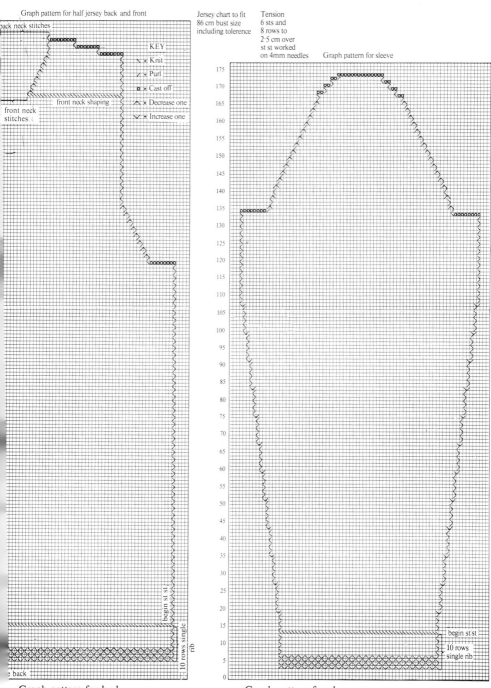

Graph pattern for half jersey back and front

back neck stitches

Jersey chart to fit
86 cm bust size
including tolerence

Tension
6 sts and
8 rows to
2·5 cm over
st st worked
on 4mm needles

Graph pattern for sleeve

KEY

↘ = Knit
↗ = Purl
□ = Cast off
△ = Decrease one
∨ = Increase one

front neck shaping

front neck
stitches

begin st st

10 rows single rib

begin st st

10 rows single rib

Graph pattern for body

Graph pattern for sleeve

garment you have in mind. Most knitting designers use graph paper at this stage, allowing one square for each stitch and one line of squares to show a complete row of knitting.

Various symbols are used to denote the different stitches and techniques and although you will not obtain a chart to the exact scale of the completed garment, it provides a visual guide which is very easy to follow.

Multiples of stitches

If you are going to adapt a pattern by using another stitch, or want to experiment for yourself, you must always take into account the exact multiples of stitches, plus any edge stitches, which are needed to ensure that the stitch will work out correctly.

Using as an example a tension of 24 stitches to 10 centimetres in width over stocking stitch, a jersey to fit an 86 centimetre bust size, allowing for 5 centimetres tolerance, will require a total of 218 stitches, divided equally between the back and the front, making 109 stitches to cast on for each of these sections.

If you want to use the turret stitch given in Chapter 5 instead of stocking stitch this requires multiples of 4 stitches plus 3 edge

stitches and will not work out exactly over 109 stitches. You must therefore decide whether to add 2 stitches making a total of 111 stitches, or subtract 2 stitches giving a total of 107 stitches, to ensure that you have the correct multiples.

Calculating quantities of yarn

There is no simple solution to this stage in adapting or designing for yourself. As explained in Chapter 1, yarn is sold by weight and not by length, so each individual quality varies in the amount contained in each ball.

The best way to begin is to buy one ball only and then knit as far as you can with this ball. You can then calculate how many balls will be needed to complete each section and estimate your total requirements. As a simple example, say you are working the back of a jersey over 100 stitches and, based on the row tension, will need 160 rows to complete this piece. If one ball will work 40 rows over the 100 stitches then you will need a total of 4 balls to complete the 160 rows.

Remember to allow for separate details, such as front bands, the neckband, pockets or any additional trimmings.

Project for advanced knitters

Adapting an existing pattern.

V-neck slipover

To fit a 56 cm chest size, allowing a further 5 cm for tolerance, plus 2 stitches for seaming.

Total quantity of yarn required, 150 g of double knitting.

Based on your own measurements and a tension of 24 stitches and 32 rows to 10 centimetres over stocking stitch worked on 4 mm needles, this design can be scaled up to fit 106 cm bust/chest size, by adding 2·4

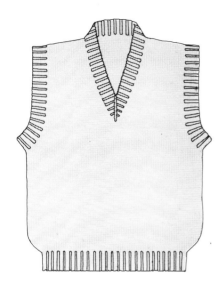

V-neck slipover

stitches and 3·2 rows for each additional centimetre difference in width and length.

Back

Using 3¾ mm needles cast on 74 sts. Work 2·5 cm single rib, or length required. Change to 4 mm needles. Beg with a K row cont in st st until work measures 20 cm from beg, or length required, ending with a P row.

SHAPE ARMHOLES

Cast off 4 sts at beg of next 2 rows. Dec one st at each end of next and every foll alt row until 60 sts rem. (Dec one-third of any additional sts at this stage.)**
Cont without shaping until armholes measure 13 cm from beg, or required length to shoulder allowing for armbands, ending with a P row.

SHAPE SHOULDERS

Cast off at beg of next and every row 6 sts 6 times. (Dec one-third of any additional sts at this stage.) Leave rem 24 sts on holder for centre back neck. (Allow rem third of any additional sts at this stage.)

Front

Work as given for back to **.

DIVIDE FOR NECK

Next row K30 sts (or half of rem sts to centre), turn and leave rem sts on holder.
Dec one st at beg of next and every foll 3rd row until 18 sts rem (or number of sts required to complete shoulder as given for back, amending shaping to every 4th row if needed).
Cont without shaping until armhole measures same as back to shoulder, ending at armhole edge.

SHAPE SHOULDER

Cast off at beg of next and every alt row 6 sts 3 times (or to match back shoulder).
With RS of work facing, rejoin yarn to rem sts and complete to match first side.

Neckband

Join right shoulder seam. Using 3¾ mm needles and with RS of work facing, K up 39 sts down left front neck (or approx 5 sts from each 6 row ends to centre), pick up loop at centre point and K tbl, mark with coloured thread to denote centre st, K up same number of sts up right front neck, then K across back neck sts on holder. 103 sts for this size. Work 2 cm single rib (or width of neckband required), dec one st at each side of centre st on every row and keeping centre st as K1 on RS rows and P1 on WS rows throughout. Cast off in rib, dec as before.

Armbands

Join left shoulder and neckband seam. Using 3¾ mm needles and with RS of work facing, K up 77 sts round armhole (or 5 sts from each 6 row ends plus cast off sts at underarm). Work in rib as given for neckband, omitting dec at centre but dec one st at each end of every row.

To make up

Press each piece as directed on ball band, omitting rib. Join side seams.

10

Completing and finishing

It is the final attention to detail, once each section of knitting has been completed, which makes the difference between a home-made and a hand-made garment. The correct pressing, seaming and trimming are essential if you are to give your garments a professional finish.

Although this is not intended as a reference book on crochet, simple edgings and trimmings in crochet can give a distinctive finish to even the plainest garment. The basic stitches in crochet are therefore included as a guide.

Blocking out and pressing

First check on a ball band of the yarn you have used to see if it requires pressing – pure acrylic yarns, for example, should never be pressed (see Chapter 1).

If pressing is recommended then each piece should be pinned out to the correct measurements given in the instructions right side down on a large, well-padded surface – an ironing board is not advised for this process. This is referred to as 'blocking'. At this stage each section can be patted into shape, making sure that the stitches and rows are straight and that the side edges are not pulled out of shape.

Once the section is pinned out, have an iron at the heat recommended for the yarn and a piece of either dry or damp cloth, as advised. Put the cloth on top of the blocked-out section, then press the whole surface of

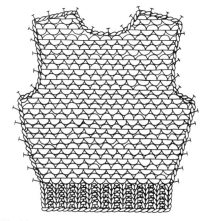

Blocking out a section

the iron down on to the cloth, lift it, then press the next area. In this way you are literally 'pressing' the fabric, and not ironing.

Pressing a section

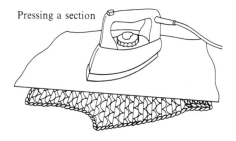

69

Remove the pins once the whole area has been pressed and put this section aside until it is required for seaming. Complete each section in this way.

Seaming

Each section is now ready to seam together in the order given in the instructions. Various methods are needed, such as a back stitch seam where any shaping has been worked, such as across the shoulders; a perfect seam, which is invisible on the right side of the work and is ideal on unshaped stocking stitch edges; or a flat seam, which should be used for garter stitch and ribbed fabrics.

Back stitch seam

This is worked with the right sides of both sections together, each seaming stitch being made one stitch in from the edge on the wrong side.

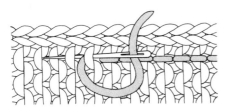

Back stitch seam

Secure the yarn with a few running stitches and work along the seam from right to left; *with the sewing needle at the back of the fabric move the width of one knitted row to the left and push the needle through to the front. Pull the yarn through but not too tightly, take the needle to the right across the front of the fabric and push it through to the back at the end of the last stitch and pull the yarn through. Repeat from the point marked with an * along the seam.

Perfect seam

This method is worked with the right sides of both sections facing you. Begin by securing the yarn to one of the pieces as given for back stitch. *Take the sewing needle across to the other section, pick up the loop of yarn which forms a bar between the edge and first stitch and pull the yarn through. Take the

Perfect seam

needle back across to the first edge and pick up the corresponding loop on this side, then pull the yarn through. Repeat from the point marked with an * along the seam.

Flat seam

Have the right sides of each section together and work from left to right. Secure the yarn as given for back stitch. Place the index finger of your left hand between the sec-

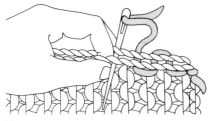

Flat seam

tions, *push the sewing needle through the edge stitch on the underside section across to the corresponding stitch on the upper section and pull the yarn through. Move along the width of one row and push the needle back through the edge of the upper section across to the corresponding stitch on the underside section and pull the yarn through. Repeat from the point marked with an * along the seam.

Picking up stitches

Once all the seams have been joined, certain sections, such as neckbands or collars, will

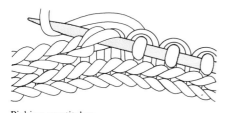

Picking up stitches

need to be completed by picking up stitches.

Unless otherwise stated in the instructions, the right side of the fabric should be facing you and the total number of stitches will be picked up with one of a pair of needles if worked in rows, or three of a set of four needles if worked in rounds. The needle and yarn should be held in the right hand in the normal way.

*Insert the point of the needle from the front to the back of the fabric one complete stitch in from the edge. Put the yarn under and over the needle, pull the loop on the needle through the fabric fairly loosely and leave it on the needle to form one stitch. Repeat from the point marked with an * until the required number of stitches has been picked up.

Trimmings

The completed garment may still need additional trimmings, such as applied embroidery or fringing. A few examples which are frequently used to enhance a knitted garment are given here.

Fringing

The yarn should be cut to twice the length of the finished fringe and one or more strands can be used, depending on the thickness required. Have the wrong side of the edge which is to be fringed facing you. Push a crochet hook through the fabric from the front to the back, fold the strand of yarn in half and put the folded loop on the hook then pull the loop through to the front of the fabric with the hook. Take the loose ends of the yarn round the hook again and pull them through the loop on the hook, then pull up these ends to tighten the knot.

71

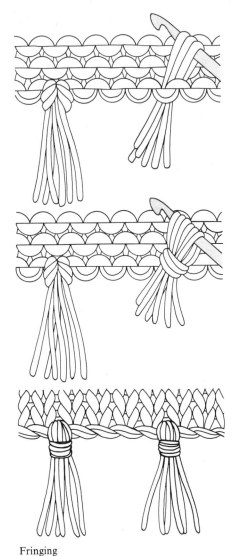

the yarn evenly round and through the centre hole until it is nearly filled, then thread the yarn into a sewing needle and use this to fill the centre hole completely.

Cut through the yarn at the outer edge of the card, working between the two pieces. Take a matching length of yarn and tie this

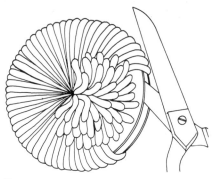

Pompons

securely round the middle of the pompon between the two pieces of card, leaving a long end for sewing on the pompon. Pull away the pieces of card and trim the pompon to shape.

Tassels

Cut a piece of card 10 centimetres wide, or the width of the finished length of the tassel.

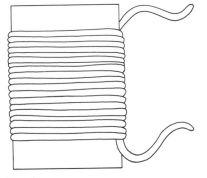

Tassels

Fringing

Pompons

Cut two pieces of card into a circle to give the finished size of the pompon, then cut a smaller circle in the centre of each piece. With the two pieces of card together wind

Wind the yarn round the card for the required thickness. Use a sewing needle threaded with a separate length of matching yarn, insert the needle along one edge of the card under all the strands, pull the needle through and pull the yarn up tightly; then fasten off. Leave an end long enough to wind round the top, folded end of the tassel several times to complete it.

Cut through the strands of yarn at the other edge of the card and trim to shape.

Swiss darning

This form of embroidery is ideal when applied to a stocking stitch fabric, as it follows the outline of each knitted stitch

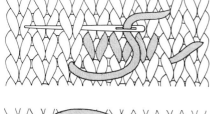

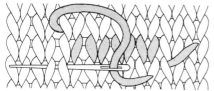

Swiss darning

exactly. The yarn used for the embroidery must be of the same thickness as the background fabric and any simple cross stitch embroidery or Fair Isle chart can be used as a motif – or see Chapter 6 for alphabet motifs.

Thread the yarn into a sewing needle and with the right side of the fabric facing you begin the embroidery at the lower right-hand edge of the design, working across the

fabric from right to left. Push the needle through from the back to the front at the bottom of the first stitch to be worked and pull the yarn through. *Take the needle under the two loops of the same stitch on the row above from right to left and pull the yarn through. Push the needle back into the same place at the base of the first stitch from the front to the back and pull the yarn through. Move the needle along to the base of the next stitch on the left, push it through from the back to the front and pull the yarn through. Repeat from the point marked with an * along the row.

At the end of the row work across the fabric from left to right, taking the needle through the base of the last stitch worked then up into the centre of this same stitch. This will now form the base of the same stitch on the row above.

Crochet trimmings

Even if you have never attempted any crochet, the basic stitches are very simple and form ideal edgings and braids.

Crochet chains

Crochet begins with a slip loop (see Chapter 2), holding the hook in the right hand and the yarn across the fingers of the left hand to achieve an even tension.

*Put the hook under and over the yarn, which should be held taut between the first and second fingers of the left hand, and catch the yarn in the curve of the hook. This is referred to as 'yarn round hook' (yrh), and is used throughout crochet stitches. Hold the slip loop between the thumb and first finger of the left hand and pull the yarn through the loop on the shank of the hook

73

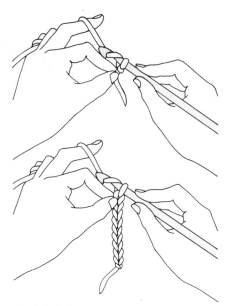

Crochet chains

To join by means of a slip stitch, as when working granny squares, push the hook through the top of the first stitch of the round from the front to the back, yarn round hook and pull the yarn through the stitch and the loop on the hook. Break off the yarn and pull it through the remaining loop on the hook to fasten off.

with the curve of the hook. One chain has been made and a working loop remains on the hook. Repeat from the point marked with an * until the required number of chains have been completed.

Crochet slip stitch

This is used as a means of getting from one position to another in a row for shaping, and also to join the last stitch of a round to the first stitch.

Crochet slip stitch join

Double crochet

This is the shallowest of crochet stitches and can also be used as a form of seaming on the right side of the fabric, working through the top of the corresponding stitches on both pieces.

The stitch can be worked over any number of chains but requires one extra chain to count as the turning chain, e.g. 11 chains are needed to make 10 double crochet.

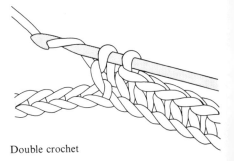

Double crochet

1st row Push the hook from the front to the back into the third chain from the hook, *yrh and draw a loop through (2 loops on hook), yrh and draw through both loops on hook. One double crochet has been completed with the 2 missed chains counting as the first double crochet. Repeat from the point marked with an * into each chain to the end. Turn the work, noting that the last stitch of the row just worked now becomes the first stitch of the next row.

2nd row 2 chain, miss the first double crochet, working under both loops at the top of the next stitch, repeat from the point marked with an * in the 1st row into each stitch to the end, working the last double crochet into the 2nd of the first 2 chain. Turn.

The 2nd row forms the pattern.

Treble crochet

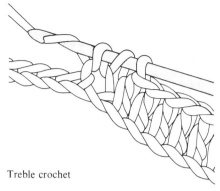

Treble crochet

This stitch can be worked over any number of chains but requires 2 extra chains to count as the turning chain, e.g. 12 chains are needed to make 10 trebles.

1st row Yrh, push the hook from the front to the back into the 4th chain from the hook, *yrh and draw a loop through (3 loops on hook), yrh and draw through 2 loops on the hook (2 loops on hook), yrh and draw through 2 loops on hook. One treble has been completed with the 3 missed chains counting as the first treble. Putting yrh to

begin each stitch, repeat from the point marked with an * into each chain to end. Turn the work as given for the 1st row of double crochet.

2nd row 3 chain, miss the first treble, working under both loops at the top of the next stitch, yrh and repeat from the point marked with an * in the 1st row into each stitch to the end, working the last treble into the 3rd of the first 3 chain. Turn.

The 2nd row forms the pattern.

Project for beginners

Working crochet granny squares.

Cot cover

62 cm wide by 82 cm long.

Total amount of yarn required, 300 g of double knitting.

One No. 4·50 crochet hook, working 4 rounds of pattern to give a square 10 cm by 10 cm.

Abbreviations: ch – chain; ss – slip stitch; sp – space; tr – treble.

Granny square

Using any colour make 6ch. Join with a ss to first ch.

1st round 3ch, working under ch work 2tr into circle, 2ch, (3tr into circle, 2ch) 3 times. Join with ss to top of first 3ch. Break off yarn.

2nd round Join next colour to any 2ch sp with ss, 3ch, work 2tr into same sp, *1ch, (3tr, 2ch, 3tr) into next 2ch sp for corner, rep from * twice more, 1ch, 3tr into same sp as beg of round, 2ch. Join with ss to top of first 3ch. Break off yarn.

3rd round Join next colour to any 2ch sp with ss, 3ch, work 2tr into same sp, *1ch, 3tr into next 1ch sp, 1ch, (3tr, 2ch, 3tr) into corner 2ch sp, rep from * twice more, 1ch, 3tr into next 1 ch sp, 1ch, 3tr into same sp as beg of round, 2ch. Join with ss to top of first 3ch. Break off yarn.

4th round Join next colour to any 2ch sp with ss, 3ch, work 2tr into same sp, *(1ch, 3tr into next 1ch sp) twice, 1ch, (3tr, 2ch, 3tr) into corner 2ch sp, rep from * twice more, (1ch, 3tr into next 1ch sp) twice, 1ch, 3tr into same sp as beg of round, 2ch. Join with ss to top of first 3ch. Fasten off.

Darn in all ends. Make 47 more squares in same way. Press as directed. Join as shown in diagram. Using any colour work 2 rounds dc round outer edge.

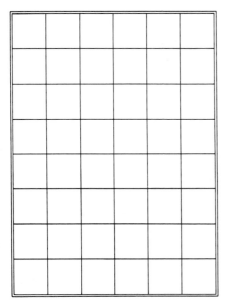

Joining granny squares for cot cover

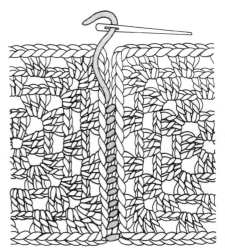

Seaming granny squares together

Part Two

Angel tops

These tops, fastening at the back or the front, are always useful and practical for a baby.

Here, the same basic shape has been used for three versions, the first with a ribbed yoke, the second with a colourful Fair Isle yoke and the third with a simple crochet edging.

(a) Angel top with ribbed yoke
(b) Angel top with Fair Isle yoke
(c) Angel top with crochet trim

Materials

(a) 4 [5] × 20 g balls of Lister Easy Wash Baby 4 ply
(b) 4 [5] × 25 g balls of Lee Target Motoravia 4 ply in main shade, A
1 [1] ball each of two contrasts, B and C
(c) 4 [5] × 20 g balls of Lister Easy Wash Baby 4 ply in main shade, A
1 [1] ball of contrast, B
One pair 3 mm needles
One pair 2¾ mm needles
One 3 mm circular Twin Pin
One 2·50 crochet hook
6 buttons

Measurements

To fit 46 [51] cm chest
Length, 24 [28] cm
Sleeve seam, 16 [18] cm

The figures given in square brackets refer to the 51 cm size only

Tension

30 sts and 38 rows to 10 cm over st st worked on 3 mm needles

(a) Angel top with ribbed yoke

(a) Front

Using 2¾ mm needles cast on 83 [93] sts. Beg with a K row work 4 rows st st.
Change to 3 mm needles.
Next row (picot row) K1, *yfwd, K2 tog, rep from * to end.
Beg with a P row cont in st st until work measures 16 [18] cm from picot row, ending with a P row.

SHAPE ARMHOLES

Cast off 2 [4] sts at beg of next 2 rows.
Next row K1, sl 1, K1, psso, K to last 3 sts, K2 tog, K1.
Next row P to end.
Rep last 2 rows 2 [5] times more. 73 sts.
Break off yarn and leave sts on holder.

79

(a) Right back

Using 2¾ mm needles cast on 43 [48] sts.
1st row K to end.
2nd row K2, P to end.
Rep these 2 rows once more.
 Change to 3 mm needles.
Next row (picot row) K1, *yfwd, K2 tog, rep from * to last 2 [3] sts, K2 [3].
Next row K2, P to end.
 Keeping 2 sts at inside edge in g st throughout, cont in st st until work measures same as front to underarm, ending with a WS row.

SHAPE ARMHOLE

Cast off 2 [4] sts at beg of next row.
Next row K2, P to end.
Next row K1, sl 1, K1, psso, K to end.
Rep last 2 rows 2 [5] times more, then first of them again. 38 sts. Break off yarn and leave sts on holder.

80

(a) Left back

Using 2¾ mm needles cast on 43 [48] sts.
1st row K to end.
2nd row P to last 2 sts, K2.
Rep these 2 rows once more.
 Change to 3 mm needles.
Next row (picot row) K2 [3] sts, *K2 tog, yfwd, rep from * to last st, K1.
Next row P to last 2 sts, K2.
 Complete to match right back, reversing shaping.

(a) Sleeves

Using 2¾ mm needles cast on 49 [53] sts. Beg first row with K1, work in K1, P1 rib for 4 cm, ending with a WS row.
 Change to 3 mm needles.
Beg with a K row cont in st st, inc one st at each end of first and every foll 6th row until there are 63 [69] sts. Cont without

shaping until sleeve measures 16 [18] cm from beg, ending with a P row.

Mark each end of last row with coloured thread and work a further 4 [6] rows, noting that these rows are set into armhole shaping.

SHAPE TOP

Next row K1, sl 1, K1, psso, K to last 3 sts, K2 tog, K1.
Next row P to end.
Rep last 2 rows 2 [5] times more. 57 sts.
Break off yarn and leave sts on holder.

(a) Yoke

Using 3 mm Twin Pin and with RS of work facing, K across sts of left back, left sleeve, front, right sleeve and right back, K2 tog at each seam. 259 sts. Cont 1n rows. K 4 rows g st. **.
Next row K2, P to last 2 sts inc one st in centre, K2. 260 sts.
Next row K3, *P4, K1, rep from * to last 2 sts, K2.
Next row K2, P1, *K4, P1, rep from * to last 2 sts, K2.
Rep last 2 rows 4 times more.
Next row K3, *P1, P2 tog, P1, K1, rep from * to last 2 sts, K2. 209 sts.
Work 7 rows rib as now set.
Next row K3, *P1, P2 tog, K1, rep from * to last 2 sts, K2. 158 sts.
Work 7 rows rib as now set.
Change to 2¾ mm needles.
Next row K3, *P2 tog, K1, rep from * to last 2 sts, K2. 107 sts.
Work 7 rows rib as now set.
Cast off in rib.

(a) To make up

Press under a dry cloth with a cool iron, omitting ribbing. Join raglan seams, sewing last 4 [6] rows of sleeve seams to cast off sts at underarm. Join side and sleeve seams. Turn hem at lower edge to WS and sl st down. Sew 6 buttons to left back and make 6 button loops on right back to correspond. Press seams.

(b) Angel top with Fair Isle yoke

(b) Front

Using 2¾ mm needles and A, cast on 83 [93] sts. K 6 rows g st.
Change to 3 mm needles. Beg with a K row cont in st st until work measures 16 [18] cm from beg, ending with a P row.

SHAPE ARMHOLES

As given for front with ribbed yoke.

(b) Right back

Using 2¾ mm needles and A, cast on 43 [48] sts. K 6 rows g st.
Change to 3 mm needles.
Next row K to end.
Next row K2, P to end.
Rep last 2 rows until work measures same as front to underarm, ending with a WS row.

SHAPE ARMHOLE

As given for right back with ribbed yoke.

(b) Left back

As given for right back, reversing g st border and all shaping.

(b) Sleeves

Using 2¾ mm needles and B, cast on 49 [53] sts. Beg first row with K1, work in K1, P1 rib for 4 cm, ending with a WS row.

Change to 3 mm needles. Break off B. Join in A. Complete as given for sleeves with ribbed yoke.

(b) Yoke

Using 3 mm Twin Pin and B, work as given for yoke of ribbed yoke to **, K3 rows g st instead of 4. Break off B. Join in A. Keeping 2 sts at each end in g st throughout, work 4 rows st st.

Next row K5 A, *2 C, 3 A, 1 C, 3 A, 2 C, 6 A, rep from * to end, ending with K5 A instead of 6 A.

Work 7 rows patt from chart.

Next row K2 A, *K2 tog A, K1 A, 1 C, 2 A, 1 C, (1 A, 1 C) twice, 2 A, 1 C, 1 A, K2 tog tbl A, rep from * to last 2 sts, K2 A. 229 sts.

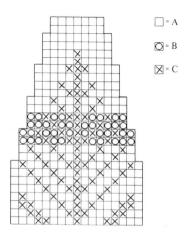

☐ = A

◯ = B

☒ = C

Work 3 rows patt from chart as now set.
Next row K2 B, *K2 tog B, (2 B, 1 C) 3 times, 2 B, K2 tog tbl B, rep from * to last 2 sts, K2 B. 199 sts.
Cont dec in this way as shown on chart on every 4th row 3 times more, then work 1 row. 109 sts.
Change to $2\frac{3}{4}$ mm needles. Join in B and K 1 row.
Next row K3, *P1, K1, rep from * to last 2 sts, K2.
Next row K2, P1, *K1, P1, rep from * to last 2 sts, K2.
Rep last 2 rows twice more, then first row again. Cast off in rib.

(b) To make up

Press under a damp cloth with a warm iron. Join as given for ribbed yoke, omitting hem.

(c) Angel top with crochet trim

(c) Back

Work as given for front with Fair Isle yoke.

(c) Left front

Work as given for right back with Fair Isle yoke.

(c) Right front

Work as given for left back with Fair Isle yoke.

(c) Sleeves

As given for sleeves with ribbed yoke.

83

(c) Yoke

Work throughout in A, as given for Fair Isle yoke, reading front for back and vice versa.

(c) Braid

Using 2·50 hook and B, make a length of ch long enough to go round lower edge of yoke, having an odd number of ch (see Chapter 10).

1st row Into 7th ch from hook work 1dc (see Chapter 10), *4ch, miss 1ch, 1dc into next ch, rep from * to end. Turn.

2nd row 6ch, 1dc into 4ch space, *4ch, 1dc into next space, rep from * to end. Fasten off.

Make 3 more strips in same way, one to fit neck edge, one more equally spaced on yoke and one for lower edge of skirt.

(c) To make up

Press and join as given for ribbed yoke, omitting hem, noting that the opening is at the centre front instead of the centre back. Sew commencing ch edge of crochet braid in place. Sew buttons to left front and make button loops on right front.

Toddler's jumper, cardigan or dressing-gown

These designs for toddlers can be varied in many different ways. The jumper can be worked in stocking stitch with just one guardsman motif worked on the centre front; the cardigan can be ribbed or the long dressing-gown version of the cardigan could feature bands of Fair Isle instead of panels of Aran pattern.

(a) Jumper
(b) Cardigan
(c) Dressing-gown

Materials

(a) 4 [5:6] × 25 g balls of Sunbeam Hyland Superwash 4 ply
(b) 4 [4:5] × 25 g balls of Sunbeam St Ives 4 ply in main shade, A
2 [2:2] balls of contrast, B
1 [1:1] ball each of two contrasts, C and D
Oddments of pink for features
(c) 9 [10:11] × 25 g balls of Sunbeam St Ives 4 ply
One pair 3¼ mm needles
One pair 2¾ mm needles
Set of four 2¾ mm needles pointed at both ends for jumper
One 3¼ mm circular Twin Pin for cardigan and dressing-gown
One 2¾ mm circular Twin Pin for cardigan and dressing-gown
5 buttons for cardigan
9 buttons for dressing-gown

Measurements

To fit 46 [51:56] cm chest
Length of jumper and cardigan, 26 [30:34] cm
Length of dressing-gown, 54 [62:70] cm
Sleeve seam, 19 [23:27] cm
The figures given in square brackets refer to the 51 and 56 cm sizes respectively

Tension

28 sts and 36 rows to 10 cm over st st worked on 3¼ mm needles

(a) Jumper

(a) Back

Using 2¾ mm needles cast on 66 [74:82] sts. Beg RS rows with P2, work 12 rows K2, P2 rib.
Change to 3¼ mm needles.
Next row (RS) P2, *K6, P2, rep from * to end.
Next row K2, *P6, K2, rep from * to end. These 2 rows form patt and are rep throughout. Cont until work measures 16 [19:22] cm from beg, ending with a WS row.

SHAPE ARMHOLES

Cast off 4 sts at beg of next 2 rows.
**Next row* K1, sl 1, K1, psso, patt to last 3 sts, K2 tog, K1.

85

Next row P2, patt to last 2 sts, P2.
Rep last 2 rows until 24 [26:28] sts rem,
ending with a WS row. Leave sts on holder
for back neck. **.

(a) Front

Work as given for back until 38 [42:46] sts
rem, ending with a WS row.

SHAPE NECK

***Next row* K1, sl 1, K1, psso, patt 10
[12:14] sts, turn and leave rem sts on holder.
Next row Patt to last 2 sts, P2.
Next row K1, sl 1, K1, psso, patt to last 2
sts, K2 tog.
Rep last 2 rows 3 [4:5] times more. 4 sts.
Cont to dec at armhole edge only on every
alt row twice more, ending with a WS row.
Cast off rem 2 sts. ***.

With RS of work facing, sl first 12 sts on
holder for centre front neck, rejoin yarn to
rem sts and patt to end.
Next row P2, patt to end.
Next row Sl 1, K1, psso, patt to last 3 sts,
K2 tog, K1.
Complete to match first side, reversing
shaping in this way.

(a) Sleeves

Using 2¾ mm needles cast on 34 [38:42] sts.
Beg RS rows with P2 [K2:P2] work 12 rows
rib as given for back.

Change to 3¼ mm needles. Beg 1st row
with P2 [K6:P2] cont in wide rib patt as
given for back, inc one st at each end of 5th
and every foll 7th row until there are 50
[58:66] sts, working extra sts into patt. Cont
without shaping until sleeve measures 19
[23:27] cm from beg, ending with a WS row.

SHAPE TOP

Cast off 4 sts at beg of next 2 rows. Work
as given for back armholes from ** to **
until 8 [10:12] sts rem.

(a) Neckband

Join raglan seams. Using set of four 2¾ mm
needles and with RS of work facing, K
across back neck and left sleeve sts on
holders K2 tog at seam, pick up and K11
[12:13] sts down left front neck, K across
front neck sts on holder, pick up and K11
[12:13] sts up right front neck, then K across
sts of right sleeve K last st of sleeve tog with
first st of back neck. 72 [80:88] sts. Cont in
rounds of K2, P2 rib for 5 cm. Cast off very
loosely in rib.

(a) To make up

Do not press. Join side and sleeve seams.
Fold neckband in half to WS and sl st down.

(b) Cardigan

(b) Back and fronts

Using 2¾ mm Twin Pin and A, cast on 130
[146:162] sts and work in one piece to
underarm. Work 12 rows rib as given for
jumper back.

Change to 3¼ mm Twin Pin. Beg with a
K row cont in rows of st st until work
measures 8 [11:14] cm from beg, ending
with a P row. Work 30 rows patt from chart.

DIVIDE FOR ARMHOLES

Next row Cont in A throughout, K28
[32:36] sts, cast off 8 sts for underarm, K58

[66:74] sts, cast off 8 sts for underarm, K to end.

Cont on last 28 [32:36] sts for left front.

Next row P to end.

Next row K1, sl 1, K1, psso, K to end.

Rep last 2 rows until 18 [20:22] sts rem, ending with a P row.

SHAPE NECK

Cont in st st throughout, work as given for jumper front from *** to ***. 5 sts rem on holder.

With WS of work facing, rejoin yarn to 58 [66:74] sts for back and P to end.

Cont in st st throughout and work as given for jumper back from ** to **.

With WS of work facing, rejoin yarn to rem 28 [32:36] sts for right front and complete to match left front, reversing shaping.

(b) Sleeves

Using $2\frac{3}{4}$ mm needles and A, cast on 34 [38:42] sts. Beg RS rows with P2, work

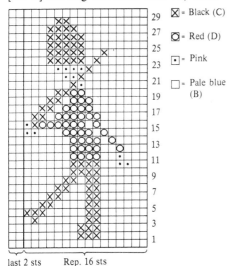

29
27
25
23
21
19
17
15
13
11
9
7
5
3
1

$\boxtimes$ = Black (C)

O = Red (D)

$\boxdot$ = Pink

$\square$ = Pale blue (B)

last 2 sts on K rows

Rep. 16 sts

first 2 sts on P rows

12 rows rib as given for jumper back.

Change to $3\frac{1}{4}$ mm needles. Beg with a K row cont in st st, inc one st at each end of 5th and every foll 8th row until there are 50 [58:66] sts, *at the same time* when work measures 11 [15:19] cm from beg, work 30 rows patt from chart, noting that the patt must be centralized.

SHAPE TOP

Cont in st st and A throughout, work as given for jumper sleeve top.

(b) Neckband

Join raglan seams. Using $2\frac{3}{4}$ mm needles, A and with RS of work facing, K across 5 sts of right front neck, pick up and K11 [12:13] sts up right front neck, K across sts of right sleeve, back neck and left sleeve, K2 tog at each back raglan seam, pick up and K11 [12:13] sts down left front neck then K across 5 sts of left front neck. 70 [78:86] sts. Beg RS rows with P2, work in K2, P2 rib for 5 cm. Cast off in rib.

(b) Right front band

Using $2\frac{3}{4}$ mm needles, A and with RS of work facing, pick up and K94 [102:110] sts from lower edge to centre of neckband. Beg RS rows with K2, work 3 rows K2, P2 rib.

Next row (buttonhole row) Rib 6, *cast off 2 sts, rib 18 [20:22], rep from * 3 times more, cast off 2 sts, rib 6.

Next row Rib to end, casting on 2 sts above those cast off in previous row.

Work 3 more rows rib. Cast off in rib.

(b) Left front band

Work as given for right front band, omitting buttonholes and beg at centre of neckband.

89

To reverse front bands for a boy, work right front band as given for left front band, and left front band as given for right front band.

(b) To make up

Press under a damp cloth with a warm iron. Join sleeve seams. Fold neckband in half to inside and sl st down. Press seams. Sew on buttons.

(c) *Dressing-gown*

(c) Back and fronts

Using 2¾ mm Twin Pin cast on 210 [226:242] sts and work in one piece to underarm. Beg with a K row work 11 rows st st. K next row to mark hemline.

Change to 3¼ mm Twin Pin. Cont in rows and patt as foll:

1st row (RS) P14 [16:18] sts, *Tw2R (see Chapter 7), patt 15 sts for panel beg with 19th row of Aran diamond and bobble patt (see Chapter 8), and rep 19th to 30th rows only throughout, Tw2L (see Chapter 7), *, P38 [42:46] sts, rep from * to *, P30 [34:38] sts, rep from * to *, P38 [42:46] sts, rep from * to *, P14 [16:18] sts.

2nd row K16 [18:20] sts, patt 15 sts for panel, K42 [46:50] sts, patt 15 sts for panel, K34 [38:42] sts, patt 15 sts for panel, K42 [46:50] sts, patt 15 sts for panel, K16 [18:20] sts.

Keeping patt correct, rep these 2 rows 11 times more.

SHAPE PANELS

25th row P12 [14:16] sts, *P2 tog, Tw2R, patt 15 sts for panel, Tw2L, P2 tog, *, P34

[38:42] sts, rep from * to *, P26 [30:34] sts, rep from * to *, P34 [38:42] sts, rep from * to *, P12 [14:16] sts.

Keeping patt correct as now set, work 11 [13:15] rows without shaping. Cont dec in this way at each side of each panel on next and every foll 12th [14th:16th] row until 130 [146:162] sts rem. Cont without shaping until work measures 45 [51:57] cm from hemline, ending with a WS row.

DIVIDE FOR ARMHOLES

Keeping patt correct throughout, work as given for cardigan.

(c) Sleeves

Using 2¾ mm needles cast on 34 [38:42] sts. Beg RS rows with P2, work 12 rows rib as given for jumper back, inc one st in centre of last row. 35 [39:43] sts.

Change to 3¼ mm needles. Commence patt as given for dressing-gown body, as foll:

Next row P8 [10:12] sts, Tw2R, patt 15 sts for panel, Tw2L, P8 [10:12] sts.

Keeping patt panel in centre correct throughout, work as given for cardigan sleeves, noting that there will be 51 [59:67] sts after inc and 9 [11:13] sts rem at end.

(c) Neckband

Work as given for cardigan neckband, dec one st in centre of each sleeve on first row.

(c) Right front band

Using 2¾ mm Twin Pin and with RS of work facing, pick up and K168 [184:200] sts from hemline to centre of neckband. Beg RS rows with K2, work 3 rows K2, P2 rib.

Next row (buttonhole row) Rib 16, *cast off 2 sts, rib 16 [18:20], rep from * 7 times more, cast off 2 sts, rib 6.

Next row Rib to end, casting on 2 sts above those cast off in previous row.

Rib 3 more rows. Cast off in rib.

(c) Left front band

Work as given for right front band, as given for cardigan left front band, noting that buttonhole row for a boy will read as foll:

Next row Rib 6, *cast off 2 sts, rib 16 [18:20], rep from * 7 times more, cast off 2 sts, rib 16.

(c) Belt

Using $2\frac{3}{4}$ mm needles cast on 11 sts. Work 70 [75:80] cm K1, P1 rib, or length required. Cast off in rib.

(c) To make up

As given for cardigan. Turn hem at lower edge to WS and sl st down.

Toddler's trousers and dungarees

Three sturdy pairs of trousers or dungarees which are both comfortable and practical.

The trousers can be made in the striped pattern given for the dungarees or trimmed with pockets, or the dungarees can be worked in one colour only.

(a) Trousers
(b) Dungarees with pockets
(c) Striped dungarees

Materials

(a) 6 [7:8] × 25 g balls of Lister Lochinvar Double Knitting
(b) 7 [8:9] × 25 g balls of Lister Superwash Double Knitting in main shade, A
1 ball of contrast, B, for pockets
Oddments for embroidery
(c) 3 [4:4] × 25 g balls of Lister Lavenda Double Knitting in main shade, A
2 [2:3] balls each of four contrasts, B, C, D and E
One pair 3¾ mm needles
One pair 3 mm needles
Waist length of elastic for trousers
2 buttons for dungarees with pockets
6 buttons for striped dungarees

Measurements

To fit 51 [56:61] cm chest
Inside leg length, 21 [24:27] cm, adjustable
The figures given in square brackets refer to the 56 and 61 cm sizes respectively

Tension

24 sts and 32 rows to 10 cm over st st worked on 3¾ mm needles

(a) Trousers

(a) Right leg

Using 3 mm needles cast on 70 [76:82] sts. Beg with a K row work 9 rows st st, then K next row to mark hemline. Change to 3¾ mm needles. Beg with a K row work 12 [16:20] rows st st.

SHAPE LEG

Dec one st at each end of next and every foll 10th row until 60 [66:72] sts rem. Cont without shaping until work measures 20 [23:26] cm from hemline, or required leg length, ending with a P row.

Inc one st at each end of next 4 rows. 68 [74:80] sts. Break off yarn and leave these sts for time being.

(a) Left leg

Work as given for right leg but do not break off yarn.

(a) To join legs

Next row Beg with left leg, K1, sl 1, K1, psso, K to last st, K last st tog with first st

93

of right leg, K across right leg sts to last 3 sts, K2 tog, K1. 133 [145:157] sts.

Beg with a P row work 3 rows.

Next row K1, sl 1, K1, psso, K to last 3 sts, K2 tog, K1.

Rep last 4 rows 4 times more. 123 [135:147] sts.

Cont without shaping until work measures 18 [20:22] cm from leg join, ending with a P row. **.

Change to 3 mm needles. Beg first row with K1, work 2·5 cm K1, P1 rib. Cast off loosely in rib.

(a) To make up

Press under a damp cloth with a warm iron. Join back seam. Join leg seams. Turn hems at lower edge of legs to WS and sl st down. Sew elastic inside waistband using herringbone casing. Press seams.

(b) Dungarees with pockets

Work as given for trousers until waist ribbing is completed but do not cast off.

DIVIDE FOR BIB

Next row Cast off 40 [46:52] sts, rib 7 and sl these sts on to holder, K29, rib 7 and sl these sts on to holder, cast off rem 40 [46:52] sts.

Using 3¾ mm needles and with WS of work facing, rejoin yarn to centre 29 sts for bib. Beg with a P row work 10 [11:12] cm st st, ending with a P row. Break off yarn and leave sts on holder. Using 3 mm needles and with WS of work facing, rejoin yarn to 2nd set of 7 sts, rib to last st, inc in last st. 8 sts.

Cont in rib until border, when slightly stretched, is same length as bib. Break off yarn and leave sts on holder.

Using 3 mm needles and with WS of work facing, rejoin yarn to other 7 sts, inc in first st, rib to end. Complete to match first border, ending with a WS row. Do not break off yarn.

Next row Rib 7, P next st tog with first st of bib, rib across bib to last st, P next st tog with first st of border, rib to end.

Work 6 rows rib across all sts.

Next row Rib 9 for first strap, cast off 25 sts, rib 9 for 2nd strap.

Cont on each set of 9 sts for 30 [33:36] cm, or required length, ending with a WS row. *Next row* (buttonhole) Rib 4, yrn, P2 tog, rib to end.

Work 1 row rib. Cast off in rib.

(b) Pockets

Using 3¾ mm needles and B, cast on 19 sts. Beg with a K row work 8 cm st st, ending with a K row. Change to 3 mm needles. K 1 row for hemline. Beg with a K row work 5 rows st st. Cast off.

Make 2 more pockets in same way.

Using oddments and Swiss darning (see Chapter 10), embroider name in centre of pockets (see alphabet in Chapter 6), or ship from chart given here.

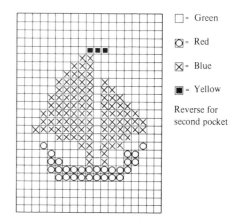

□ = Green

Ø = Red

⊠ = Blue

■ = Yellow

Reverse for second pocket

(b) To make up

As given for trousers. Sew borders to sides of bib. Sew on 2 buttons to back waist. Sew on pockets.

(c) *Striped dungarees*

Work as given for trousers to **, working hem in A then after hemline row change to 3¾ mm needles and work 4 rows g st with A. Cont in striped patt of 6 rows st st, 4 rows g st, 6 rows st st, 2 rows g st, 6 rows st st and 6 rows g st, rep these 30 rows throughout and working in striped sequence of B, C, D, E and A throughout.

DIVIDE FOR BODY

Next row (R S facing) Break off yarn, sl first 34 [37:40] sts on to holder, rejoin yarn and K55 [61:67] sts, turn and leave rem 34 [37:40] sts on holder.

Cont in striped patt on centre sts for 8 [8·5:9] cm, ending with a W S row. Cast off 2 sts at beg of next 14 [16:18] rows. Leave rem 27 [29:31] sts on holder.

With R S of work facing, return to sts which were left, sl first 6 sts at each end of front on to holders for borders, then with back seam in centre, rejoin yarn and K across rem sts, K2 tog in centre. 55 [61:67] sts.

Complete to match front.

FRONT BORDERS

Mark positions for 2 buttonholes on each side of front, first to come just below beg of top shaping and the second halfway between this one and the division of the work. Sl one set of 6 sts on to 3 mm needles. Using A and with R S of work facing work as foll:

Next row K1, P1, K1, pick up loop lying between needles and P tbl, K1, P1, K1.
Cont in rib on these 7 sts, making buttonholes as markers are reached, as foll:
Next row (buttonhole) Rib 3, yfwd, K2 tog, P1, K1.

Cont in rib until band, when slightly stretched, reaches to top of front, ending with a W S row. Leave these sts on holder. Work second border to match.
***Next row* Rib 6, K next st tog with first st of front, K across front sts to last st, K last st tog with first st of other border, rib to end.

Work 6 rows rib across all sts. ***. Cast off in rib.

BACK BORDERS AND STRAPS

Using 3 mm needles and A, cast on 7 sts. Work in rib until back borders measure same as front borders, omitting buttonholes, ending with a W S row. Work a second border in same way.
Work as given for front from *** to ***.

DIVIDE FOR STRAPS

Next row Rib 9, cast off 21 [23:25] sts, rib to end.
Cont on each set of 9 sts in rib for 15 [16:17] cm, or required length, ending with a W S row.
Next row (buttonhole) Rib 4, yrn, P2 tog, rib to end.
Cont in rib, dec one st at each end of next 3 rows. K3 tog. Fasten off.

(c) To make up

As given for trousers. Sew borders to back and front, sewing cast on edges of back borders behind beg of front borders. Press seams. Sew on buttons.

Child's sweater, pullover and cardigan

A classic range for children; as shown here in stocking stitch they are ideal for school wear.

You can vary these basic shapes by introducing all-over patterning, or bands of contrast colours; panels of Aran or cable stitches would also look effective. See Chapter 9 for planning your own design.

(a) Sweater
(b) Pullover
(c) Cardigan

Materials

(a) 10 [11:12:13:14:15] × 25 g balls of Hayfield Gaylon 4 ply
(b) 9 [10:11:12:13:14] balls of same
(c) 10 [11:11:12:13:14] balls of same
One pair 3¼ mm needles
One pair 2¾ mm needles
Set of four 2¾ mm needles pointed at both ends for sweater or pullover
5 [5:5:6:6:6] buttons for cardigan

Measurements

To fit 61 [66:71:76:81:86] cm chest
Length, 38 [42:46:50:54:58] cm, adjustable
Sleeve seam, 31 [33:36:38:41:43] cm, adjustable
The figures given in square brackets refer to the 66, 71, 76, 81 and 86 cm sizes respectively

Tension

28 sts and 36 rows to 10 cm over st st worked on 3¼ mm needles

(a) Sweater

(a) Back

Using 2¾ mm needles cast on 91 [97:105:111:119:125] sts. Beg first row with K1, work 4 cm K1, P1 rib, ending with a WS row.

Change to 3¼ mm needles. Beg with a K row cont in st st until work measures 25 [28:31:34:37:40] cm from beg, or required length to underarm, ending with a P row.

SHAPE ARMHOLES

Cast off 8 sts at beg of next 2 rows. 75 [81:89:95:103:109] sts.
**Next row K1, sl 1, K1, psso, K to last 3 sts, K2 tog, K1.
Next row P to end. **.
Rep last 2 rows until 29 [31:35:37:41:43] sts rem, ending with a P row. Leave rem sts on holder for back neck.

(a) Front

Work as given for back until 49 [51:57:59:65:67] sts rem, ending with a P row.

Next row K1, sl 1, K1, psso, K16 [16:18:18:20:20] sts, turn and leave rem sts on holder.

Next row P to end.

Next row K1, sl 1, K1, psso, K to last 3 sts, sl 1, K1, psso, K1.

Next row P to end.

Rep last 2 rows 6 [6:7:7:8:8] times more. 4 sts. Cont dec at armhole edge only on next and foll alt row. Cast off rem 2 sts.

With RS of work facing, sl first 11 [13:15:17:19:21] sts on to holder for centre front neck, rejoin yarn to rem sts, K to last 3 sts, K2 tog, K1.

Next row P to end.

Next row K1, K2 tog, K to last 3 sts, K2 tog, K1.

Complete to match first side, reversing shaping as shown.

(a) Sleeves

Using 2¾ mm needles cast on 45 [47:49:51:53:55] sts. Work 4 cm rib as given for back, ending with a WS row.

Change to 3¼ mm needles. Beg with a K row cont in st st, inc one st at each end of 7th and every foll 8th row until there are 67 [71:75:79:83:87] sts. Cont without shaping until sleeve measures 31 [33:36:38:41:43] cm from beg, or required length to underarm, ending with a P row. Mark each end of last row with coloured thread. Work 10 more rows st st, noting that these 10 rows are set into armhole shaping and are not included in sleeve seam measurements.

Work as given for back from ** to ** until 53 sts rem, ending with a P row.

Next row K1, sl 1, K1, psso, K21, K2 tog, K1, sl 1, K1, psso, K21, K2 tog, K1.

Cont dec in this way in centre on every

foll 6th row 4 times more, *at the same time* cont dec at each end of every alt row as before until 11 sts rem, ending with a P row. Leave sts on holder.

(a) Polo collar or crew neckband

Join raglan seams, sewing last 10 rows of sleeves from markers to cast off sts at under-arm.

Using set of four 2¾ mm needles and with RS of work facing, K across sts of back neck and left sleeve K2 tog at seam, pick up and K14 [16:17:19:20:22] sts down side of neck, K across front neck sts, pick up and K14 [16:17:19:20:22] sts up other side of neck, then K across sts of right sleeve K last st of sleeve tog with first st of back neck. 88 [96:104:112:120:128] sts.

Cont in rounds of K1, P1 rib for 15 [15:18:18:21:21] cm for polo collar, or 4 [4:4:5:5:5] cm for crew neckband. Cast off loosely in rib. Fold polo collar to RS. Fold crew neckband in half to WS and sl st down.

(a) To make up

Press under a damp cloth with a warm iron. Join side and sleeve seams. Press seams.

(b) Pullover

(b) Back

Work as given for sweater back.

(b) Front

Work as given for back to underarm, ending with a P row.

Cast off 8 sts at beg of next 2 rows.

Next row K1, sl 1, K1, psso, K34 [37:

41 : 44 : 48 : 51] sts, turn and leave rem sts on holder.

Next row P to end.

Next row K1, sl 1, K1, psso, K to last 3 sts, sl 1, K1, psso, K1.

Next row P to end.

Next row K1, sl 1, K1, psso, K to end.

Next row P1, P2 tog tbl, P to end.

Next row K1, sl 1, K1, psso, K to end.

Rep last 6 rows until 12 [13:15:16:18:19] sts have been dec at neck edge, then cont dec at armhole edge only on every alt row until 2 sts rem, ending with a P row. Cast off.

With RS of work facing, sl first st on to holder for centre front neck, rejoin yarn to rem sts, K to last 3 sts, K2 tog, K1.

Next row P to end.

Next row K1, K2 tog, K to last 3 sts, K2 tog, K1.

Next row P to end.

Next row K to last 3 sts, K2 tog, K1.

Next row P to last 3 sts, P2 tog, P1.

Next row K to last 3 sts, K2 tog, K1.

Complete to match first side, reversing shaping as shown.

(b) Sleeves

Work as given for sweater sleeves.

(b) Neckband

Join raglans as given for sweater.

Using set of four 2¾ mm needles and with RS of work facing, K across sts of back neck and left sleeve K2 tog at seam, pick up and K40 [44:47:51:54:58] sts down left front neck, K centre front st, pick up and K40 [44:47:51:54:58] sts up right front neck, then K across sts of right sleeve K last st of sleeve tog with first st of back neck. 130 [140:150:160:170:180] sts.

Next round Work in K1, P1 rib to 2 sts before centre front st, P2 tog, K1, P2 tog tbl, rib to end.

Rep this round 6 [6:7:7:8:8] times more. Cast off in rib, still dec as before.

(b) To make up

As given for sweater.

(c) Cardigan

(c) Back

Work as given for sweater back but cast off rem sts.

(c) Left front

Using 2¾ mm needles cast on 43 [45:49:53:57:59] sts. Work 4 cm rib as given for back, ending with a WS row and inc one st in centre of last row on 2nd, 3rd and 6th sizes only. 43 [46:50:53:57:60] sts.

Change to 3¼ mm needles. Beg with a K row cont in st st until work measures 4 rows less than back to underarm, ending with a P row.

SHAPE FRONT EDGE

Next row K to last 3 sts, sl 1, K1, psso, K1. Beg with a P row work 3 rows.

SHAPE ARMHOLE

Next row Cast off 8 sts, K to last 3 sts, sl 1, K1, psso, K1.

Next row P to end.

Next row K1, sl 1, K1, psso, K to end.

Next row P to end.

Next row K1, sl 1, K1, psso, K to last 3 sts, sl 1, K1, psso, K1.

Rep last 4 rows 7 [8:10:11:13:14] times more. 9 [9:7:7:5:5] sts. Cont to dec at armhole edge only on every alt row until 2 sts rem, ending with a P row. Cast off.

(c) Right front

Work as given for left front, reversing all shaping.

(c) Sleeves

Work as given for sweater sleeves but cast off rem sts.

(c) Border

Mark positions for buttonholes on right front edge for a girl, or left front edge for a boy, first to come in centre of welt and last to come approx 2 cm below beg of front shaping, with 3 [3:3:4:4:4] more evenly spaced between.

Using $2\frac{3}{4}$ mm needles cast on 9 sts. Beg first row with K1, work in rib as given for back for 2 cm, ending with a WS row.

Next row (buttonhole) Rib 4, cast off 2 sts, rib to end.

Next row Rib 3, cast on 2 sts, rib to end.

Make 4 [4:4:5:5:5] more buttonholes in same way as markers are reached. Cont in rib until band is long enough to fit up front, round neck and down other front, when slightly stretched. Cast off in rib.

(c) To make up

Press and join raglans as given for sweater. Join side and sleeve seams. Sew on border. Press seams. Sew on buttons.

Jersey, slipover and cardigan for men or women

Just three variations on classic shapes are shown here but they can be varied in many other ways.

Work the jersey and slipover in cable panels or plain stocking stitch, or adapt one of the stitches given in the technical chapters.

The cardigan can be made in all-over Fair Isle pattern, with bands of Fair Isle or with just pockets highlighted with a Fair Isle or Swiss embroidered motif.

(a) Polo jersey
(b) Slipover
(c) Cardigan

Materials

(a) 19 [20:21:22] × 25g balls of Wendy Double Knitting in main shade, A
1 [1:2:2] balls each of two contrasts, B and C
(b) 6 [6:7:7] balls of same in main shade, A
4 [4:4:5] balls of contrast, B
3 [3:3:4] balls of contrast, C
3 [3:4:4] balls of contrast, D
(c) 21 [22:23:24] balls of same
One pair 3¾mm needles
One pair 3mm needles
One 3¾mm circular Twin Pin
One 3mm circular Twin Pin
Set of four 3mm needles pointed at both ends for jersey and slipover

Cable needle for cardigan
7 buttons for cardigan

Measurements

To fit 81 [89:97:104] cm bust
Length, 59 [61:63:65] cm
Sleeve seam, 43 [44:45:46] cm
The figures given in square brackets refer to the 89, 97 and 104 cm sizes respectively

Tension

24 sts and 32 rows to 10 cm over plain stocking stitch worked on 3¾ mm needles

(a) Polo jersey

(a) Body

Using 3 mm Twin Pin and A, cast on 208 [224:240:256] sts and work in one piece to underarm. Work in rounds of K1, P1 rib for 5 cm.

Change to 3¾ mm Twin Pin. Using A, K 2 rounds st st. Cont in rounds of st st, working Shetland or Fair Isle patt which has multiples of 16 sts from chart (see Chapter 6). When border has been completed, noting that one extra row is required to complete any Shetland patt, cont using A only until

work measures 41 cm from beg, or required length to underarm, ending at end of round.

DIVIDE FOR ARMHOLES

Next round Cast off 5 sts for first part of underarm, K95 [103:111:119] sts for front, cast off 9 sts for underarm, K95 [103:111:119] sts for back, cast off 4 sts for underarm. Break off yarn.

Using 3¾ mm needles and with WS of work facing, rejoin yarn to sts for back. P 1 row.

Cast off 2 sts at beg of next 4 rows. Dec one st at each end of next and foll 3 [4:5:6] alt rows. 79 [85:91:97] sts. Cont without shaping until armholes measure 18 [20:22:24] cm, ending with a P row.

SHAPE SHOULDERS

Cast off at beg of next and every row 6 [6:7:7] sts 6 times and 5 [7:6:8] sts twice. Leave rem 33 [35:37:39] sts on holder for back neck.

With WS of work facing, rejoin yarn to sts for front. Work as given for back until armholes measure 13 [15:17:19] cm from beg, ending with a P row.

**SHAPE NECK

Next row K32 [34:36:38] sts, turn and leave rem sts on holder.

Cast off 2 sts at beg of next and foll alt row, then dec one st at neck edge on foll 5 alt rows. 23 [25:27:29] sts. Cont without shaping until armhole measures same as back to shoulder, ending with a P row.

SHAPE SHOULDER

Cast off at beg of next and every alt row 6 [6:7:7] sts 3 times and 5 [7:6:8] sts once.

With RS of work facing, sl first 15 [17:19:21] sts on to holder for centre front neck, rejoin yarn to rem sts and K to end.

106

Complete to match first side, reversing shaping.

(a) Sleeves

Using 3 mm needles and A, cast on 49 [51:53:55] sts. Beg first row with K1, work 5 cm K1, P1 rib, ending with a WS row and inc 4 [6:8:10] sts evenly across last row. 53 [57:61:65] sts.

Change to 3¾ mm needles. Beg with a K row work 2 rows st st, then work the border patt as given for body, noting that the patt must be centralized. When border is completed, cont using A only, inc one st at each end of 2nd and every foll 8th row until there are 75 [79:83:87] sts. Cont without shaping until sleeve measures 43 [44:45:46] cm from beg, ending with a WS row.

SHAPE TOP

Cast off 5 sts at beg of next 2 rows. Dec one st at each end of next and foll 13 [14:15:16] alt rows, ending with a WS row. 37 [39:41:43] sts. Cast off at beg of next and every row 2 sts 8 [8:10:10] times, 3 sts 4 times and 9 [11:9:11] sts once.

(a) Collar

Join shoulder seams. Using set of four 3 mm needles, A and with RS of work facing, K across back neck sts on holder, pick up and K20 sts down left front neck, K across front neck sts on holder then pick up and K20 sts up right front neck. 88 [92:96:100] sts.

Cont in rounds of K1, P1 rib for 15 cm for polo collar. Cast off loosely in rib.

Crew neckband can be worked in same way for 5 cm, folding neckband to WS and sl st down, noting that 1 ball less yarn may be required.

(a) Pockets

Using 3¾ mm needles and A, cast on 21 sts. Work 4 rows st st. Work border patt as given for body over centre 17 sts, keeping 2 sts at each end in A throughout. When border is completed, using A work 4 rows st st.
Change to 3 mm needles. K1 row to mark fold line. Beg with a K row work 5 rows st st. Cast off.
Make another pocket in same way.

(a) To make up

Press each piece under a damp cloth with a warm iron. Join sleeve seams. Set in sleeves. Fold pocket tops to WS and sl st down. Sew one pocket to top of each sleeve in centre. Press seams.

(b) Slipover

(b) Body

Cast on and work rib as given for polo jersey body.
Change to 3¾ mm Twin Pin. Using A, K 1 round st st. Cont in rounds of st st, working Shetland or Fair Isle patt which has multiples of 16 sts from chart (see Chapter 6), until work measures 37 cm from beg, or required length to underarm, ending at end of round.

DIVIDE FOR ARMHOLES

Next round To ensure that patt is centralized for back and front, cast off 9 [5:8:5] sts for first part of underarm, patt 95 [103:111:119] sts for front, cast off 9 sts for underarm, patt 95 [103:111:119] sts for back, cast off 0 [4:1:4] sts for underarm. Break off yarn.
Using 3¾ mm needles and with WS of work facing, rejoin yarn to sts for back and keeping patt correct throughout, complete as given for polo jersey back, noting that armholes should measure 22 [24:26:28] cm from beg instead of 18 [20:22:24] cm.
With WS of work facing, rejoin yarn to sts for front. Work as given for back until armholes measure 8 [10:12:14] cm from beg, ending with a WS row.
Complete as given for polo jersey front from ** to end.

(b) Neckband

Join shoulder seams. Using set of four 3 mm needles, A and with RS of work facing, K across back neck sts on holder, pick up and K 36 sts down left front neck, K across front neck sts on holder, then pick up and K 36 sts up right front neck. 120 [124:128:132] sts. Cont in rounds of K1, P1 rib for 2 cm. Cast off in rib.

(b) Armbands

Using set of four 3 mm needles, A and with RS of work facing, pick up and K 120 [128:136:144] sts round armhole. Work in rounds of K1, P1 rib for 2 cm. Cast off in rib.

(b) To make up

Press as given for polo jersey.

(c) Cardigan

(c) Body

Using 3 mm Twin Pin cast on 209 [223:239:253] sts. Beg first row with P1, work in K1, P1 rib for 5 cm, ending with a WS row and inc one st in centre of last row on 2nd and 4th sizes only. 209 [224:239:254] sts.

107

Change to 3¾ mm Twin Pin. Commence patt.

1st row P4 [5:6:7] sts, *K6, P9 [10:11:12], rep from * 12 times more, K6, P4 [5:6:7].
2nd row K4 [5:6:7] sts, *P6, K9 [10:11:12], rep from * 12 times more, P6, K4 [5:6:7].
Rep these 2 rows once more.
5th row P4 [5:6:7] sts, *C6B (see Chapter 7), P9 [10:11:12], rep from * 12 times more, C6B, P4 [5:6:7].

Cont in patt as now set, working cables on every 8th row, until work measures 41 cm from beg, or required length to underarm, ending with a WS row.

DIVIDE FOR ARMHOLES

Next row Patt 48 [52:56:60] sts, cast off 8 sts for underarm, patt 97 [104:111:118], cast off 8 sts, patt to end.

Cont on last 48 [52:56:60] sts for left front. Patt 1 row. Cast off 2 sts at beg of next and foll alt row. Dec one st at armhole edge on foll 3 [4:5:6] alt rows. 41 [44:47:50] sts.

Cont without shaping until armhole measures 13 [15:17:19] cm from beg, ending with a WS row.

SHAPE NECK

Next row Patt 35 [37:39:41] sts, turn and leave rem 6 [7:8:9] sts on holder.

Cast off 3 sts at beg of next row and 2 sts at beg of foll 2 alt rows. Dec one st at neck edge on next and foll 4 alt rows. Cont without shaping until armhole measures 18 [20:22:24] cm from beg, ending with a WS row.

SHAPE SHOULDER

Cast off at beg of next and every alt row 6 [6:7:7] sts 3 times and 5 [7:6:8] sts once.

With WS of work facing, rejoin yarn to 97 [104:111:118] sts for back and patt to end. Cast off 2 sts at beg of next 4 rows, then dec one st at each end of next and foll 2 [3:4:5] alt rows. 83 [88:93:98] sts.

Cont without shaping until armholes measure same as front to shoulder, ending with a WS row.

SHAPE SHOULDERS

Cast off at beg of next and every row 6 [6:7:7] sts 6 times and 5 [7:6:8] sts twice. Leave rem 37 [38:39:40] sts on holder for back neck.

With WS of work facing, rejoin yarn to rem sts for right front and complete to match left front, reversing shaping.

(c) Sleeves

Using 3 mm needles cast on 49 [51:53:55] sts. Beg 1st row with P1, work in K1, P1 rib for 5 cm, inc 4 [5:6:7] sts evenly across last row. 53 [56:59:62] sts.

Change to 3¾ mm needles. Commence patt.

1st row P1, *K6, P9 [10:11:12], rep from * twice more, K6, P1.

Cont in patt as now set, working cables on 5th and every foll 8th row, *at the same time* inc one st at each end of 5th and every foll 8th row until there are 75 [80:85:90] sts, working extra sts into reversed st st. Cont without shaping until sleeve measures 43 [44:45:46] cm from beg, ending with a WS row.

SHAPE TOP

Cast off 4 sts at beg of next 2 rows. Dec one st at each end of next and foll 13 [14:15:16] alt rows, ending with a WS row. 39 [42:45:48] sts. Cast off at beg of next and every row 2 sts 8 [10:10:12] times, 3 sts 4 times and 11 [10:13:12] sts once.

(c) Left front band

Using 3 mm needles cast on 10 sts. Beg 1st row with P1, work in K1, P1 rib until band, when slightly stretched, fits along left front edge, ending with a WS row. Break off yarn and leave sts on holder.

Tack band in place and mark positions for 7 buttons, the first to come in centre of welt and the last to come 1 cm up in centre of neckband, with 5 more evenly spaced between.

(c) Right front band

Using 3 mm needles cast on 10 sts. Beg 1st row with K1, work in rib as given for left front band, making buttonholes on RS row as markers are reached, as foll:

Next row (buttonhole row) Rib 4, cast off 3 sts, rib to end.

Next row Rib to end, casting on 3 sts above those cast off in previous row.

(c) Neckband

Join shoulder seams. Using 3 mm needles and with RS of work facing, rib across first 9 sts of right front band, P next st tog with first st of neck sts on holder, K across rem 5 [6:7:8] front neck sts, pick up and K20 sts up right front neck, K across back neck sts dec one st in centre on 2nd and 4th sizes only, pick up and K20 sts down left front neck, K5 [6:7:8] front neck sts on holder, P next st tog with first st of left front band, rib across rem 9 sts of left front band. 107 [109:113:115] sts.

Cont in rib for 4 cm, making buttonhole as before after 1 cm has been worked, then another after 3 cm has been worked to form double buttonhole. Cast off loosely in rib.

(c) To make up

Press as given for polo jersey. Join sleeve seams. Set in sleeves. Sew on front bands. Fold neckband in half to WS and sl st down, sewing round double buttonhole. Press seams. Sew on buttons.

Chunky jackets and an over-jersey

Variations on simple shapes make these chunky jackets or an over-jersey. The body is just two squares which can be joined at the centre back and front, or side seams; the sleeves and yoke are worked as two more pieces and the hood is optional.

(a) Hooded jacket
(b) Patterned jacket
(c) Striped over-jersey

Materials

(a) 28 [29:30:31:32] × 25 g balls of Sirdar Superwash Double Knitting in main shade, A
5 [5:5:6:6] balls each of two contrasts, B and C
(b) 15 [16:16:17:17] balls of same in main shade, A
13 [13:14:14:15] balls of contrast, B
(c) 5 [5:6:6:6] balls each of same in five contrasts, A, B, C, D and E
4 [4:4:5:5] balls each of any two of the colours for edging
One pair 4 mm needles
One 3·50 crochet hook
6 toggles for hooded jacket

Measurements

To fit 86 [91:97:102:107] cm bust
Length, 80 [81:82:83:84] cm
Sleeve seam, 43 [44:45:46:47] cm

The figures given in square brackets refer to the 91, 97, 102 and 107 cm sizes respectively

Tension

22 sts and 40 rows to 10 cm over g st worked on 4 mm needles; approximately 36 rows over turret st

(a) Hooded jacket

(a) Body

Using 4 mm needles and A, cast on 114 sts for right half of body and work from side edge to side edge. Work 42 [45:48:51:54] cm g st. Cast off.
Work left half of body in same way.

(a) Sleeves

Using 4 mm needles and A, cast on 70 [74:78:82:86] sts. Work 48 [49:50:51:52] cm g st.

SHAPE NECK EDGE

Next row K29 [30:31:32:33] sts, turn and leave rem sts on holder.
Dec one st at beg of next and foll 5 alt rows, then at same edge on every foll 4th row 5 times more. 18 [19:20:21:22] sts. Cont without shaping until work measures 10 cm from beg of neck shaping. Cast off.

Return to sts which were left, rejoin yarn and cast off centre 12 [14:16:18:20] sts, K to end.

Complete to match first side, reversing shaping.

Make another sleeve in same way.

(a) Hood

Using 4 mm needles and A, cast on 70 sts. Work 45 [46:47:48:49] cm g st. Cast off.

(a) Crochet edging

BODY

Using 3·50 crochet hook, A and with R S of one piece of body facing, work in dc round all edges (see Chapter 10), working approx 3 dc into every 4 sts, 3 dc into every 8 rows (4 ridges of g st), and working 3 dc into each corner. Join with a ss to first dc (see Chapter 10). Fasten off.

2nd round With R S of work facing, join in B to any st and work in half trebles – called htr –, right round (putting yrh to beg, insert hook into st, yrh and draw loop through, yrh and draw through all 3 loops on hook for each htr), and working 3 htr into each corner. Join with a ss to first htr. Fasten off.

BEGINNERS IN CROCHET. Cont working 4 more rounds of htr inc at corners on every round, using C and B alt. Fasten off.

ADVANCED CROCHETERS. Cont in foll patt, working in htr throughout and inc at corners on every round, adjusting patt as required and noting that the colour not in use is laid along the top of the sts and worked over with the colour in use, so that the work is reversible.

3rd round Join in C, work (1 C, 3 B) all round.

4th round Work (2 C, 2 B) all round.

5th round Work (3 C, 1 B) all round.

6th round Work in C all round. Fasten off.

Work other piece in same way.

SLEEVES

Work as given for body, inc at each outer corner on each round and dec round curve of neck as required, to ensure that neck edge lies flat.

HOOD

Fold work in half and join top seam, noting that cast on and cast off edges form face edge.

Work round face edge only as given for body.

(a) To make up

Do not press. All seams, except neck edge, are joined with dc in C, working through two thicknesses.

Join centre back seam of body. Join back yoke seam of sleeves. Place centre-back seam to back yoke seam and join as far as centre of body pieces, which will be the equivalent of the side seams, then join rem part of body pieces to front yoke. Join underarm seams.

Stitch neck edge of hood to neck edge of body.

Make 3 ch loops in any colour and join into a figure 8 to form toggle fasteners. Sew on toggles.

(b) Patterned jacket

(b) Body

Using 4 mm needles and A, cast on 123 sts for right half of body and work from side edge to side edge. Work in turret s (see Chapter 5), for 49 [52:55:58:61] cm, end-

ing with a 1st or 9th patt row. Cast off.
Work left half of body in same way.

(b) Sleeves

Using 4 mm needles and A, cast on 87 [91 : 95 : 99 : 103] sts. Work in turret st for 52 [53 : 54 : 55 : 56] cm.

SHAPE NECK EDGE

Next row Patt 37 [38 : 39 : 40 : 41] sts, turn and leave rem sts on holder.

Dec one st at beg of next and foll 11 alt rows. 25 [26 : 27 : 28 : 29] sts. Cont without shaping until work measures 10 cm from beg of neck shaping. Cast off.

Return to sts which were left, rejoin yarn and cast off centre 13 [15 : 17 : 19 : 21] sts, patt to end. Complete to match first side, reversing shaping.

Make another sleeve in same way.

(b) To make up

With R S facing, join pieces tog as given for hooded jacket, but sew instead of crocheting, and omit hood.

Using 3·50 hook, A and with R S of work facing, work 1 row dc round all edges (see Chapter 10). Turn and work 2 rows htr; see edging for hooded jacket.

Using 3·50 hook and B, make lengths of crochet ch for ties (see Chapter 10), and sew in pairs to front edges.

(c) Striped over-jersey

(c) Body and sleeves

As given for hooded jacket, working throughout in g st and striped patt of 4 rows each in A, B, C, D and E.

(c) Crochet edging

Using 3·50 hook and colours as required, work edging as given for hooded jacket.

(c) To make up

Do not press. The body pieces form the back and front and are joined at the side seams.

Using last colour used for edging, crochet sections tog as given for hooded jacket, joining yoke to top edges of body.

If required, make a pair of ties as given for patterned jacket and sew to each front corner of neck.

Long wrapover jackets

These long-line women's jackets are warm and practical; with easy raglan sleeves and a tie belt they could take the place of a winter coat.

(a) Plain jacket
(b) Jacket with Fair Isle motifs
(c) Jacket with patterned panels

Materials

(a) 22 [23:25:26] × 50 g balls of Emu Fiord
(b) 22 [23:25:26] balls of same in main shade, A
1 [1:1:1] ball of contrast, B
(c) 23 [24:26:27] balls of same
One pair 5½ mm needles
One pair 4½ mm needles
One 4½ mm circular Twin Pin, 100 cm long

Measurements

To fit 86 [91:97:102] cm bust
Length, 91 [93:95:97] cm
Sleeve seam, 43 [44:45:46] cm
The figures given in square brackets refer to the 91, 97 and 102 cm sizes respectively

Tension

16 sts and 22 rows to 10 cm over st st worked on 5½ mm needles. Check your tension very carefully

(a) *Plain jacket*

(a) Back

Using 4½ mm needles cast on 87 [91:95:99] sts. Beg with a K row work 9 rows st st, then K next row to mark hemline.
Change to 5½ mm needles. Beg with a K row, work 32 rows st st. **.

SHAPE BACK

Next row K3, sl 1, K1, psso, K26 [27:28:29], sl 1, K1, psso, K21 [23:25:27], K2 tog, K26 [27:28:29], K2 tog, K3.
Beg with a P row work 23 rows.
Next row K3, sl 1, K1, psso, K24 [25:26:27], sl 1, K1, psso, K21 [23:25:27], K2 tog, K24 [25:26:27], K2 tog, K3.
Cont dec in this way on every foll 24th row twice more. 71 [75:79:83] sts. Cont without shaping until work measures 72 cm from hemline, ending with a P row.

SHAPE ARMHOLES

Cast off 3 sts at beg of next 2 rows.
Next row K2, sl 1, K1, psso, K to last 4 sts, K2 tog, K2.
Next row P to end.
Rep last 2 rows until 21 sts rem, ending with a P row.
Leave sts on holder for back neck.

(a) Left front

Using 4½ mm needles cast on 57 [59:61:63] sts and work as given for back to **.

SHAPE FRONT

Next row K3, sl 1, K1, psso, K26 [27:28:29], sl 1, K1, psso, K to end.
Beg with a P row work 23 rows.
Next row K3, sl 1 K1, psso, K24 [25:26:27], sl 1, K1, psso, K to end.
Cont dec in this way on every foll 24th row twice more. 49 [51:53:55] sts. Cont without shaping until work measures 40 rows less than back to underarm, ending with a P row.

SHAPE FRONT EDGE

Next row K to last 3 sts, K2 tog, K1. Beg with a P row work 3 rows.
Rep last 4 rows 9 times more.

SHAPE ARMHOLE

Next row Cast off 3 sts, K to last 3 sts, K2 tog, K1.
Next row P to end.
Next row K2, sl 1, K1, psso, K to end.
Next row P to end.
Next row K2, sl 1, K1, psso, K to last 3 sts, K2 tog, K1.
    Rep last 4 rows 9 times more, then cont to dec at armhole edge only on every alt row until 4 sts rem, ending with a P row.
Next row K2, sl 1, K1, psso.
Next row P3.
Leave these 3 sts on holder.

(a) Right front

Work as given for left front, reversing all shaping.

(a) Sleeves

Using 4½ mm needles cast on 33 [35:37:39] sts. Beg with a K row work 9 rows st st, then K next row to mark hemline.
    Change to 5½ mm needles. Beg with a K row cont in st st, inc one st at each end of 11th and every foll 8th row until there are 51 [55:59:63] sts. Cont without shaping until sleeve measures 43 [44:45:46] cm from hemline, ending with a P row.

SHAPE TOP

Cast off 3 sts at beg of next 2 rows. Work 2 rows st st. Dec one st as given for back at each end of next and every foll 4th row twice more, then at each end of every alt row until 7 sts rem, ending with a P row. Leave sts on holder.

(a) Front border

Join raglan seams. Using 4½ mm Twin Pin and with RS of work facing, pick up and K104 sts from hemline to beg of neck shaping on right front, 70 [73:76:79] sts to top of right front, K across sts on holders for right front, right sleeve, back neck, left sleeve and left front, K2 tog at each raglan seam, pick up and K70 [73:76:79] sts down left front to beg of neck shaping, then K104 sts to hemline. 385 [391:397:403] sts.
Turn and cont working in rows. Beg first row with P1, work 6 rows K1, P1 rib. Cast off in rib.

(a) Belt

Using 4½ mm needles cast on 9 sts. Work in K1, P1 rib for 130 cm, or required length. Cast off in rib.

(a) To make up

Press each piece under a damp cloth with a warm iron, omitting ribbing. Join side and

sleeve seams. Fold hems at lower edge and cuffs to W S and sl st down. Press seams.

(b) Jacket with Fair Isle motifs

Work back and fronts as given for plain jacket.

(b) Sleeves

Work as given for plain jacket sleeves until sleeve measures 10 cm from hemline.

Cont as given for plain version, working a band of Fair Isle pattern with A and B from any of the Fair Isle charts given in Chapter 6. Note that the pattern must be centralized and the inc sts worked into patt when possible.

When patt band is completed, cont as given for plain jacket sleeves, using A only.

(b) Pockets

Using 5½ mm needles and A, cast on 23 sts. Beg with a K row work 2 rows st st.

Work Fair Isle patt rows as given for sleeve, keeping 3 sts at each end in A. Using A only P 1 row st st, inc one st at each end of row. Change to 4½ mm needles. Beg first row with P1, work 4 rows K1, P1 rib. Cast off in rib.

Make another pocket in same way.

(b) Front border and belt

Work as given for plain jacket.

(b) To make up

Work as given for plain jacket. Sew on pockets.

(c) Jacket with patterned panels

(c) Back

Cast on and work hemline as given for plain jacket.

Change to 5½ mm needles. Cont as given for plain jacket over patt panels, as foll:
1st row K14, *Tw2R (see Chapter 7), K6 [7:8:9] and work in ladder patt on these sts (see Chapter 8), Tw2L (see Chapter 7), *, K9, Tw2R, K17 [19:21:23] and work in diamond patt on these sts keeping 2 [3:4:5] at each side in st st (see Chapter 8), Tw2L, K9, rep from * to *, K14.
2nd row Work in patt as set.
3rd row As 1st row but over centre 17 [19:21:23] sts of diamond patt work K8 [9:10:11], P1, K8 [9:10:11].

Keeping patt panels correct as now set cont until 32 rows have been worked from hemline.

SHAPE BACK

Next row K3, sl 1, K1, psso, K9, patt 10 [11:12:13] sts, K7, sl 1, K1, psso, patt 21 [23:25:27] sts, K2 tog, K7, patt 10 [11: 12:13] sts, K9, K2 tog, K3.

Keeping patt correct as set, complete as given for plain jacket back.

(c) Left front

Cast on and work hemline as given for plain jacket left front.

Change to 5½ mm needles. Cont as given for plain jacket over patt panels to match back of this version, as foll: *1st row* K14, Tw2R, K6 [7:8:9], Tw2L, K9, Tw2R, K17 [19:21:23], Tw2L, K3 [2:1:0].

(c) Right front

Work as given for left front, reversing all shaping and noting that 1st patt row will read as foll:

1st row K3 [2:1:0], Tw2R, K17 [19:21:23], Tw2L, K9, Tw2R, K6 [7:8:9], Tw2L, K14.

(c) Sleeves

Cast on 33 [37:41:45] and work hemline as given for plain jacket sleeve.

Change to 5½ mm needles. Work as given for plain jacket sleeves noting that 1st patt row will read as foll:

1st row K1, *Tw2R, K6 [7:8:9] for ladder patt, Tw2L, *, K11 [13:15:17] and keep these sts in st st throughout, rep from * to *, K1.

Complete as given for plain jacket sleeve, working inc sts into st st.

(c) Front border, belt and making up

As given for plain jacket.

124

Zipped jacket and an Aran cardigan and jersey for men or women

These designs are suitable for a man or woman. The zip-fronted jacket could feature panels of Aran pattern as given for the cardigan, or the jersey and cardigan can be worked throughout in stocking stitch.

(a) Zipped jacket
(b) Aran cardigan
(c) Aran jersey

Materials

(a) 12 [12:13:14:14] × 50 g balls of 3 Suisses Gailic Bainin
(b) 14 [15:15:16:17] balls of same
(c) 13 [13:14:15:16] balls of same
One pair 5 mm needles
One pair 4 mm needles
Set of four 4 mm needles for jersey
Cable needle for cardigan and jersey
6 buttons for cardigan
55 [55:60:60:60] cm open-ended zip fastener for jacket
Lining for pockets

Measurements

To fit 91 [97:102:107:112] cm bust/chest
Length, 64 [66:68:70:72] cm, adjustable
Sleeve seam, 44 [45:46:47:48] cm, adjustable
The figures given in square brackets refer to the 97, 102, 107 and 112 cm sizes respectively

Tension

16 sts and 22 rows to 10 cm over st st worked on 5 mm needles

(a) Zipped jacket

(a) Back

Using 4 mm needles cast on 81 [85:89:93:97] sts. Beg 1st row with K1, work in K1, P1 rib for 5 cm, ending with a WS row. **.

Change to 5 mm needles. Beg with a K row cont in st st until work measures 42 cm from beg, or required length to underarm ending with a P row.

SHAPE ARMHOLES

Cast off 4 sts at beg of next 2 rows.
***Next row K1, K2 tog, K to last 3 sts, sl 1, K1, psso, K1.
Next row P to end. ***.
Rep last 2 rows until 27 sts rem, ending with a P row. Leave sts on holder for back neck.

(a) Left front

Using 4 mm needles cast on 41 [43:45:47:49] sts.
1st row *K1, P1, rep from * to last 3 sts, K3.
2nd row K2, P1, *K1, P1, rep from * to end.

125

Rep these 2 rows for 5 cm ending with a 2nd row.

Change to 5 mm needles.

Next row K to end.

Next row K2, P to end.

Rep last 2 rows until work measures 10 cm from beg, ending with a WS row.

DIVIDE FOR POCKET OPENING

Next row K14 [14:16:16:18] sts, turn and leave rem sts on holder.

Beg with a P row cont in st st on these sts for a further 12 cm, ending with a K row. Break off yarn and leave sts on holder.

With RS of work facing, rejoin yarn to rem 27 [29:29:31:31] sts and keeping 2 sts at front edge in g st throughout cont in st st for a further 12 cm, ending with a K row. *Next row* K2, P25 [27:27:29:29] sts, then P across 14 [14:16:16:18] sts on holder. Cont in st st across all sts until work measures same as back to underarm, ending with a WS row.

SHAPE ARMHOLE

Cast off 4 sts at beg of next row.

Next row K2, P to end.

Next row K1, K2 tog, K to end.

Rep last 2 rows until 24 sts rem, ending with a WS row.

SHAPE NECK

Next row K1, K2 tog, K16, turn and leave rem 5 sts on holder.

****Next row* P to end.

Next row K1, K2 tog, K to last 3 sts, sl 1, K1, psso, K1.

Rep last 2 rows 6 times more. 4 sts. Cont to dec at armhole edge only on foll 2 alt rows. Cast off rem 2 sts. ****.

(a) Right front

Using 4 mm needles cast on 41 [43:45:47:49] sts.

1st row K3, *P1, K1, rep from * to end.

2nd row *P1, K1, rep from * to last 3 sts, P1, K2.

Complete to match left front, reversing all shaping and position of pocket.

(a) Sleeves

Using 4 mm needles cast on 33 [37:41:45:49] sts. Work 5 cm rib as given for back ending with a WS row.

Change to 5 mm needles. Beg with a K row cont in st st, inc one st at each end of 9th and every foll 8th row until there are 51 [55:59:63:67] sts. Cont without shaping until sleeve measures 44 [45:46:47:48] cm from beg, or required length to underarm ending with a P row.

*****Mark each end of last row then work a further 6 rows, noting that these rows are set into armhole shaping and are not included in sleeve seam measurement.

SHAPE TOP

Work as given for back from *** to *** until 5 sts rem, ending with a WS row. Leave sts on holder.

(a) Neckband

Join raglan seams, sewing last 6 rows of sleeve seams to cast off sts at underarm on body.

Using 4 mm needles and with RS of work facing, K across 5 sts of right front neck, pick up and K12 sts up right front neck, K across sts of right sleeve, back neck and left sleeve K2 tog at each back raglan seam, pick up and K12 sts down left front neck then K across 5 sts of left front neck. 69 sts.

Next row K2, *P1, K1, rep from * to last 3 sts, P1, K2.

Next row K3, *P1, K1, rep from * to last 2 sts, K2.

Rep last 2 rows for 5 cm. Cast off loosely in rib.

(a) Pocket edges

Using 4 mm needles and with R S of work facing, pick up and K25 sts along outer edge of pocket.
Next row (WS) K1, *P1, K1, rep from * to end.
Next row P1, *K1, P1, rep from * to end.
Rep last 2 rows for 2·5 cm.
Cast off in rib.

(a) To make up

Press under a damp cloth with a warm iron. Join side and sleeve seams. Sew in zip to come halfway up neckband. Fold neckband in half to inside and sl st down. Sew down pocket edges. Cut out pockets from lining and sew in place to inner edge of pockets and outer edge where sts were picked up. Press seams.

(b) Aran cardigan

(b) Back

Work as given for zipped jacket back to ** but beg R S rows with P1.
Change to 5 mm needles. Commence patt.
1st row (P1, K1) 7 [7:8:8:9] times for Irish moss st, *P1, (K1, K twice into next st, K1) making 4 sts for cable panel, (P5, K twice into next st, P1, K twice into next st, P5) making 15 sts for Aran diamond panel (see Chapter 8), (K1, K twice into next st, K1) making 4 sts for cable panel, P1, *, K1, (P1, K1) 5 [7:7:9:9] times for Irish moss st, rep

from * to *, (K1, P1) to end for Irish moss st. 89 [93:97:101:105] sts.
2nd row (K1, P1) 7 [7:8:8:9] times, *K1, P4 for cable panel, (K5, P2, K1, P2, K5) as 2nd row of Aran diamond patt, P4 for cable panel, K1, *, P1, (K1, P1) 5 [7:7:9:9] times, rep from * to *, (P1, K1) to end.
3rd row (K1, P1) 7 [7:8:8:9] times, *P1, C4B (see Chapter 7), (P4, Cb, K1, Cf, P4) as 3rd row of Aran diamond patt, C4F (see Chapter 7), P1, *, P1, (K1, P1) 5 [7:7:9:9] times, rep from * to *, (P1, K1) to end.
4th row (P1, K1) 7 [7:8:8:9] times, *K1, P4 for cable panel, (K4, P2, K1, P1, K1, P2, K4) as 4th row of Aran diamond, P4 for cable panel, K1, *, K1, (P1, K1) 5 [7:7:9:9] times, rep from * to *, (K1, P1) to end.
Cont in patt as now set, noting that C4B is worked at beg of each panel and C4F at end on every 6th row and that rows 1 to 20 only are worked throughout over 15 sts for Aran diamond panel.
Keeping patt correct throughout, complete as given for zipped jacket back, casting off 5 sts instead of 4 at armholes and working W S rows of shaping as foll:
Next row P2, patt to last 2 sts, P2.
When 33 sts rem instead of 27 sts, cast off for back neck.

(b) Left front

Using 4 mm needles cast on 39 [41:43:45:47] sts. Beg R S rows with P1, work 5 cm K1, P1 rib, ending with a W S row.
Change to 5 mm needles. Commence patt.
1st row (P1, K1) 7 [7:8:8:9] times for Irish moss st, work from * to * as given for 1st row of Aran cardigan back, (K1, P1) 2 [3:3:4:4] times for Irish moss st. 43 [45:47:49:51] sts.

Cont in patt as now set until work measures 10 cm from beg, ending with a WS row.

Next row Patt 14 [14:16:16:18] sts, turn and leave rem sts on holder.

Keeping patt correct throughout complete this side of pocket opening as given for zipped jacket left front.

With RS of work facing rejoin yarn to rem 29 [31:31:33:33] sts. Keeping patt correct throughout and omitting g st front edge complete pocket opening as given for zipped jacket left front.

Cont in patt until work measures 8 rows less than back to underarm, ending with a WS row.

Next row Patt to last 3 sts, sl 1, K1, psso, K1.
Work 3 rows patt without shaping.
Rep last 4 rows once more.

Next row Cast off 5 sts, patt to last 3 sts, sl 1, K1, psso, K1.

Cont to dec at front edge on every foll 4th row 10 times more, *at the same time* dec at armhole edge on every alt row to match back until 2 sts rem, ending with a WS row. Cast off.

(b) Right front

Work as given for left front, reversing patt, shaping and position of pocket opening and noting that 1st patt row will read as foll:
1st row (P1, K1) 2 [3:3:4:4] times, work from * to * as given for 1st row of Aran cardigan back, (K1, P1) 7 [7:8:8:9] times.

(b) Sleeves

Using 4 mm needles cast on 33 [37:41:45:49] sts. Beg 1st row with P1, work 5 cm K1, P1 rib, ending with a WS row.
Change to 5 mm needles. Commence patt.
1st row (P1, K1) 3 [4:5:6:7] times, work from * to * as given for 1st row of back, (K1, P1) to end. 37 [41:45:49:53] sts.

Cont in patt as now set, inc one st at each end of 9th and every foll 8th row and working extra sts into Irish moss st, until there are 55 [59:63:67:71] sts. Cont without shaping until sleeve measures 44 [45:46:47:48] cm from beg, or required length to underarm, ending with a WS row.

Complete as given for zipped jacket sleeves from ***** to end until 9 sts rem instead of 5 sts. Cast off.

(b) Front border

Using 4 mm needles cast on 9 sts. Beg RS rows with P1, work 2·5 cm K1, P1 rib.
Next row (buttonhole row) Rib 3, cast off 3 sts, rib to end.
Next row Rib 3, cast on 3 sts, rib to end.

Make 5 more buttonholes in same way at intervals of 6·5 cm, then cont in rib until band is long enough to fit up front edge, round sleeve tops and neck edge and down other front. Cast off.

(b) Pocket edges

Work as given for zipped jacket pocket edges.

(b) To make up

As given for zipped jacket. Sew on front border. Sew on buttons.

(c) Aran jersey

(c) Back

Work as given for zipped jacket back to **,
dec one st in centre of last row. 80
[84:88:92:96] sts.
Change to 5 mm needles. Commence
patt.
1st row (P1, K1) 7 [7 : 8 : 8 : 9] times for Irish
moss st, *P2, (K twice into next st) making
2 sts for Tw2R (see Chapter 7), P2, (K3, pick
up loop lying between sts and K tbl, K3)
making 7 sts for lobster claw st (see Chapter
8), P2, (K twice into next st) making 2 sts
for Tw2L (see Chapter 7), P2, *, P20
[24:24:28:28] sts for trinity st (see Chapter
8), rep from * to *, (K1, P1) to end for Irish
moss st. 86 [90:94:98:102] sts.
2nd row (K1, P1) 7 [7:8:8:9] times, *K2, P2,
K2, P7 for lobster claw st, K2, P2, K2, *,
(P3 tog, K1, P1, K1 all into next st) 5
[6:6:7:7] times as given for 2nd row of
trinity st, rep from * to *, (P1, K1) to end.
3rd row (K1, P1) 7 [7 : 8 : 8 : 9] times, *P2,
Tw2R, P2, cable 7 sts as given for 3rd row
of lobster claw st, P2, Tw2L, P2, *, P20
[24:24:28:28] sts, rep from * to *, (P1, K1)
to end.
4th row (P1, K1) 7 [7 : 8 : 8 : 9] times, rep from
* to * on 2nd row, (K1, P1, K1 all into next
st, P3 tog) as given for 4th row of trinity st,
rep from * to *, (K1, P1) to end.
Cont in patt as now set and complete as
given for zipped jacket back, working WS
rows of shaping as foll:
Next row P2, patt to last 2 sts, P2.
When 32 sts rem instead of 27 sts, leave
sts on holder for back neck.

(c) Front

Work as given for back until front measures
10 cm from beg, ending with a WS row.

DIVIDE FOR POCKET OPENINGS

Next row Patt 14[14:16:16:18] sts, turn and
leave rem sts on holder.
Cont in patt on these sts for a further
12 cm, ending with a RS row. Break off yarn
and leave sts on holder.
With RS of work facing, rejoin yarn to
rem sts.
Next row Patt 58 [62:62:66:66] sts, turn and
leave rem sts on holder.
Cont in patt on these sts for a further
12 cm, ending with a RS row. Break off yarn
and leave sts on holder.
With RS of work facing, rejoin yarn to
rem 14 [14:16:16:18] sts and patt to end.
Cont in patt on these sts for a further
12 cm, ending with a RS row.
Next row Patt 14 [14:16:16:18] sts, patt
across 58 [62:62:66:66] sts on holder then
patt across 14 [14:16:16:18] sts on holder.
Cont in patt across all sts as given for
Aran jersey back until 52 sts rem, ending
with a WS row.

SHAPE NECK

Next row K1, K2 tog, patt 16 sts, turn and
leave rem sts on holder.
Keeping patt correct, complete as given for
zipped jacket left front from **** to ****.
With RS of work facing, sl first 14 sts on
to holder for centre front neck, rejoin yarn
to rem sts, patt to last 3 sts, sl 1, K1, psso,
K1.
Complete to match first side.

(c) Sleeves

Using 4 mm needles cast on 33 [37:
41 : 45 : 49] sts and work 5 cm rib as given for
back, ending with a WS row.
Change to 5 mm needles. Commence
patt.
1st row (P1, K1) 4 [5 : 6 : 7 : 8] times for Irish
moss st, P2, (K twice into next st) making

131

2 sts for Tw2R, P2, K7 for lobster claw st, P2, (K twice into next st) making 2 sts for Tw2L, P2, (K1, P1) to end for Irish moss st. 35 [39:43:47:51] sts.

Keeping patt correct as now set, inc one st at each end of 9th and every foll 8th row until there are 53 [57:61:65:69] sts, working extra sts into Irish moss st.

Complete as given for zipped jacket sleeves, dec until 7 sts rem instead of 5 sts.

(c) Neckband

Join raglan seams as given for zipped jacked neckband.

Using set of four 4 mm needles and with R S of work facing, K across sts of back neck and left sleeve K 2 tog at seam, pick up and K12 sts down left front neck, K across front neck sts, pick up and K12 sts up right front neck, then K across sts of right sleeve K last st of sleeve tog with first st of back neck. 82 sts. Cont in rounds of K1, P1 rib for 5 cm. Cast off loosely in rib.

(c) Pocket edges

As given for zipped jacket pocket edges.

(c) To make up

As given for zipped jacket, omitting zip.

132

Zip-fronted battle jackets for men or women

Three versions of a battle jacket shape with raglan sleeves, suitable for a man or a woman.

(a) Plain jacket, with optional pockets
(b) Striped jacket
(c) Patchwork jacket

Materials

(a) 17 [18:19:20:21] × 25 g balls of Patons Superwash Double Knitting in main shade, A
1 ball of contrast, B, for pockets and embroidery
(b) 10 [11:12:13:14] balls in main shade, A
3 [3:4:4:4] balls each of three contrasts, B, C and D
(c) 6 [6:7:7:8] balls in main shade, A
4 [4:5:5:5] balls each of four contrasts, B, C, D and E
One pair 3¾ mm needles
One pair 3 mm needles
One 3¾ mm circular Twin Pin
One 3 mm circular Twin Pin 50 [50:55:55:55] cm open-ended zip fastener

Measurements

To fit 86 [91:97:102:107] cm bust/chest
Length, 56 [57:58:59:60] cm
Sleeve seam, approx 45 cm

The figures given in square brackets refer to the 91, 97, 102 and 107 cm sizes respectively

Tension

24 sts and 32 rows to 10 cm over st st worked on 3¾ mm needles

(a) Plain jacket, with optional pockets

(a) Body

Using 3 mm Twin Pin and A, cast on 215 [227:239:251:263] sts and work in one piece to underarm. Beg first row with P1, work 8 cm K1, P1 rib, ending with a WS row and inc one st in centre of last row.

Change to 3¾ mm Twin Pin. Beg with a K row cont in st st until work measures 37 cm from beg, ending with a P row.

DIVIDE FOR ARMHOLES

Next row K48 [51:54:57:60] sts, cast off 12 sts for underarm, K96 [102:108:114:120], cast off 12 sts, K to end.
Cont on last 48 [51:54:57:60] sts for left front.
Next row P to end.
Next row K1, sl 1, K1, psso, K to end.

133

Rep last 2 rows until 27 [28:29:30:31] sts rem, ending with a P row.

Next row K1, sl 1, K1, psso, K17, turn and leave rem 7 [8:9:10:11] sts on holder.
Next row P to end.
Next row K1, sl 1, K1, psso, K to last 2 sts, K2 tog.
Rep last 2 rows 7 times more, ending with a P row. 3 sts.
Next row K1, sl 1, K1, psso.
Cast off rem 2 sts.

With WS of work facing, rejoin yarn to 96 [102:108:114:120] sts for back and P to end.
Next row K1, sl 1, K1, psso, K to last 3 sts, K2 tog, K1.
Next row P to end.
Cont dec in this way on next and every alt row until 34 [36:38:40:42] sts rem, ending with a P row. Leave rem sts on holder for back neck.

With WS of work facing, rejoin yarn to rem 48 [51:54:57:60] sts for right front and P to end.
Next row K to last 3 sts, K2 tog, K1.
Complete to match left front, reversing shaping.

(a) Sleeves

Using 3 mm needles and A, cast on 45 [47:49:51:53] sts. Work 4 cm K1, P1 rib as given for body, ending with a WS row and inc one st in centre of last row. Change to $3\frac{3}{4}$ mm needles. Beg with a K row cont in st st, inc one st at each end of 7th and every foll 8th row until there are 72 [74:76:78:80] sts, then at each end of every 6th row until there are 74 [78:82:86:90] sts.

Cont without shaping until sleeve measures approx 47·5 cm from beg, ending with a P row, and noting that last 8 rows

are set into armhole shaping and are not included in sleeve seam measurements.

Next row K1, sl 1, K1, psso, K to last 3 sts, K2 tog, K1.
Next row P to end.
Rep last 2 rows until 36 sts rem, ending with a P row.
Next row K1, sl 1, K1, psso, K13, sl 1, K1, psso, K2 tog, K13, K2 tog, K1.

Cont dec in this way in centre of every foll 8th row twice more, *at the same time* cont dec at each end of every alt row as before until 6 sts rem, ending with a P row. Leave rem sts on holder.

(a) Neckband

Join raglan seams, sewing last 8 rows of sleeve seams to cast off sts at underarms. Using 3 mm needles, A and with RS facing, K across 7 [8:9:10:11] sts of right front neck, pick up and K14 sts up side of neck, K across sts of right sleeve, back neck and left sleeve, K2 tog at each back raglan seam and at centre back neck, pick up and K14 sts down side of neck then K across rem sts of left front neck. 85 [89:93:97:101] sts.

Beg first row with K1, work 5 cm K1, P1 rib. Cast off loosely in rib.

(a) Pockets

Using $3\frac{3}{4}$ mm needles and B, cast on 30 sts. Beg with a K row work 2 rows st st. Keeping 3 extra sts at each end in B throughout, work Patch No. 2 as given in Chapter 6, then work 2 more rows st st with B.

Change to 3 mm needles and A. K 1 row inc one st in centre. Work 6 rows K1, P1 rib. Cast off in rib. If required, Swiss darn name in centre of pocket (see Chapter 6 for alphabet).

Make another pocket in same way.

(a) To make up

Press under a damp cloth with a warm iron. Join sleeve seams. Using 3 mm needles, A and with RS of work facing, pick up and K135 [138:141:144:147] sts up right front edge to centre of neckband, then cast off knitwise. Work along left front edge in same way. Sew in zip. Fold neckband in half to WS and sl st down. Sew on pockets. Press seams.

(b) Striped jacket

Work throughout as given for plain version, omitting pockets. Work ribbed welt, cuffs, neckband and front edges in A.
Work main sections throughout in 12 rows striped patt, as foll: 2 rows A, 2 rows B, 2 rows A, 2 rows C, 2 rows A, 2 rows D. Note that sleeve top shaping should beg on same striped row as underarm shaping on body.

(c) Patchwork jacket

Work throughout as given for plain version, omitting pockets. Work ribbed welt, cuffs, neckband and front edges in A.
Work main sections throughout in st st and patchwork, as foll:

FIRST, THIRD AND FIFTH SIZES

Work patches across entire width as given in Chapter 6 in any order and colour sequence at random.

SECOND AND FOURTH SIZES

Work patches as given in Chapter 6, see first, third and fifth sizes, but keep 6 sts in A at each front edge throughout.

ALL SIZES

Arrange patches on sleeves so that they change in the centre, working any extra sts and increased sts into patt when possible. You may find it helpful to chart the sts out first on graph paper (see Chapter 9).

Man's sweater, waistcoat or cardigan

Three variations on a theme; you could just as easily work the band of Fair Isle across the body of the waistcoat, or work the patterned sleeves and pockets on the cardigan, omitting the Fair Isle.

(a) Sweater with saddle shoulders
(b) Waistcoat
(c) Cardigan with bands of Fair Isle across yoke and sleeves

Materials

(a) 24 [25:26:27] × 25 g balls of Robin Rusticana
(b) 18 [19:19:20] × 25 g balls of Robin Vogue Double Knitting
(c) 22 [23:24:25] × 25 g balls of Robin Vogue Double Knitting in main shade, A
2 [2:2:2] balls of contrast, B
1 [1:2:2] balls of contrast, C
1 [1:1:1] ball each of two contrasts, D and E
One pair 3¾ mm needles
One pair 3 mm needles
Set of four 3 mm needles pointed at both ends for sweater and waistcoat
One 3¾ mm and one 3 mm circular Twin Pin for waistcoat and cardigan
6 buttons for waistcoat and cardigan

Measurements

To fit 97 [102:107:112] cm chest

Length, 64 [65:66:67] cm
Sleeve seam, 45 [46:47:48] cm
The figures given in square brackets refer to the 102, 107 and 112 cm sizes respectively

Tension

24 sts and 32 rows to 10 cm over st st worked on 3¾ mm needles

(a) Sweater with saddle shoulders

(a) Back

Using 3 mm needles cast on 121 [129:137:145] sts. Beg with a K row work 11 rows st st, then K next row to mark hemline. **.

Change to 3¾ mm needles. Beg with a K row cont in st st until work measures 43 cm from hemline, ending with a P row. ***.

SHAPE ARMHOLES

Cast off at beg of next and every row 4 sts twice and 2 sts 4 times.
Next row K1, sl 1, K1, psso, K to last 3 sts, K2 tog, K1.
Next row P to end.
Rep last 2 rows 4 [6:8:10] times more. 95 [99:103:107] sts. Cont without shaping

137

until armholes measure 17 [18:19:20] cm from beg, ending with a P row.
Next row Cast off 30 [31:32:33] sts, K to last 30 [31:32:33] sts, cast off rem sts.
Leave rem 35 [37:39:41] sts on holder for back neck.

(a) Front

Work as given for back until armholes measure 13 [14:15:16] cm from beg, ending with a P row.

SHAPE NECK

Next row K36 [37:38:39] sts, turn and leave rem sts on holder.
Next row P to end.
Next row K to last 3 sts, sl 1, K1, psso, K1.
Next row P to end.
Rep last 2 rows 5 times more.
Cast off rem 30 [31:32:33] sts.

With RS of work facing, sl first 23 [25:27:29] sts on to holder for centre front neck, rejoin yarn to rem sts and K to end.

Complete to match first side, reversing shaping.

(a) Sleeves

Using 3 mm needles cast on 47 [51:55:59] sts and work as given for back to **. Change to 3¾ mm needles. Cont in patt.
1st row K3, *P1, K3, rep from * to end.
2nd row K1, P1, *K3, P1, rep from * to last st, K1.
Rep 1st and 2nd rows twice more.
7th row As 2nd row.
8th row As 1st row.
Rep 7th and 8th rows twice more.
Rep these 12 rows throughout, inc one st at each end of next and every foll 8th row, working extra sts into patt, until there are 79 [83:87:91] sts. Cont without shaping until sleeve measures 45 [46:47:48] cm from hemline, ending with a WS row.

SHAPE TOP

Cast off 4 sts at beg of next 2 rows.
Next row K1, sl 1, K1, psso, patt to last 3 sts, K2 tog, K1.
Next row P2, patt to last 2 sts, P2.
Rep last 2 rows 13 [14:15:16] times more. 43 [45:47:49] sts.
Cast off at beg of next and every row 2 sts 6 [4:8:6] times and 3 sts 4 [6:4:6] times. 19 sts.

SADDLE SHOULDER TOP

Cont on rem sts for length of shoulder on back and front, ending with a WS row. Leave sts on holder.

(a) Neckband

Sew saddle shoulder tops to body shoulders. Using set of four 3 mm needles and with RS of work facing, K across sts of back neck and left sleeve on holders K2 tog at seam, pick up and K12 sts down left front neck, K across front neck sts on holder, pick up and K12 sts up right front neck, K across sts of right sleeve on holder, K last st of sleeve tog with first st of back neck. 118 [122:126:130] sts.

Cont in rounds of K1, P1 rib for 6 cm. Cast off loosely in rib. Fold neckband in half to WS and sl st down.

(a) Pockets

Using 3¾ mm needles cast on 31 sts. Work 13 cm patt as given for sleeves, ending with a WS row. Change to 3 mm needles. P 1 row to mark hemline. Beg with a P row work 7 rows st st. Cast off.

Make another pocket in same way.

(a) To make up

Press under a damp cloth with a warm iron. Set in sleeves. Join side and sleeve seams.

Turn hems at lower edge, cuffs and pockets to WS and sl st down. Sew on pockets. Press seams.

(b) Waistcoat

(b) Body

Using 3 mm Twin Pin cast on 241 [257:273:289] sts and work in one piece in rows as given for sweater back to ***.

****DIVIDE FOR ARMHOLES

Next row K56 [60:64:68] sts, cast off 8 sts for underarm, K113 [121:129:137], cast off 8 sts, K to end.

Cont on last 56 [60:64:68] sts for left front.

Next row P to end.
Next row Cast off 2 sts, K to end.
Next row P to end.
Rep last 2 rows once more.
Next row K1, sl 1, K1, psso, K to last 3 sts, sl 1, K1, psso, K1.
Next row P to end.
Next row K1, sl 1, K1, psso, K to end.
Next row P1, P2 tog tbl, P to end.

Cont to dec at armhole edge on next and foll 2 [4:6:8] alt rows, *at the same time* cont to dec at front edge on every 3rd row as shown until 28 [29:30:31] sts rem. Cont without shaping until armhole measures 21 [22:23:24] cm from beg, ending at armhole edge.

SHAPE SHOULDER

Cast off at beg of next and every alt row 7 [7:8:8] sts 3 times and 7 [8:6:7] sts once.

With WS of work facing, rejoin yarn to 113 [121:129:137] sts for back and P to end. Cast off 2 sts at beg of next 4 rows.

Next row K1, sl 1, K1, psso, K to last 3 sts, K2 tog, K1.

140

Next row P to end.
Rep last 2 rows 4 [6:8:10] times more. 95 [99:103:107] sts.
Cont without shaping until armholes measure 21 [22:23:24] cm from beg, ending with a P row.

SHAPE SHOULDERS

Cast off at beg of next and every row 7 [7:8:8] sts 6 times and 7 [8:6:7] sts twice. Cast off rem 39 [41:43:45] sts.

With WS of work facing, rejoin yarn to rem 56 [60:64:68] sts for right front and P to end. Complete to match left front, reversing shaping.

(b) Front border

Mark positions for 6 buttonholes on left front, first to come 2 cm above hemline and last to come 2 cm below beg of front shaping, with 4 more evenly spaced between.

Using 3 mm needles cast on 10 sts. Beg every row with K1, work 2 cm K1, P1 rib.
Next row Rib 4, cast off 2 sts, rib to end.
Next row Rib 4, cast on 2 sts, rib to end.

Cont in rib, making 5 more buttonholes in same way as markers are reached, then cont until band is long enough to fit up front edge from hemline, round neck and down other front edge to hemline. Cast off.

(b) Armhole bands

Join shoulder seams. Using set of four 3 mm needles and with RS of work facing, pick up and K146 [154:162:170] sts round armholes. Work in rounds of K1, P1 rib for 2 cm. Cast off in rib.

(b) Pockets

Work as given for sweater pockets, but working in st st throughout instead of patt.

(b) To make up

Press as given for sweater. Turn hem at lower edge and pockets to WS and sl st down. Sew on front border. Sew on pockets. Press seams. Sew on buttons.

(c) Cardigan with Fair Isle bands

(c) Body

Using 3 mm Twin Pin and A, work as given for waistcoat body to ***, *at the same time* when work measures 37 cm from hemline, work 19 rows of Fair Isle patt from chart given in Chapter 6, noting that if you use a Fair Isle patt from the same chapter which has a different number of rows, the length must be adjusted accordingly, so that when the patt is completed the work will measure 43 cm from hemline.

Using A throughout, complete as given for waistcoat from **** to end.

(c) Sleeves

Using 3 mm needles and A, cast on 47 [51:55:59] sts and work as given for sweater sleeves, working in st st throughout instead of patt. When sleeve measures 39 [40:41:42] cm from hemline, work band of Fair Isle patt as given for cardigan body, noting that the patt must be centralized. You may find it helpful to chart the sts out first on graph paper (see Chapter 9).

SHAPE TOP

Work as given for sweater sleeve until 19 sts rem. Cast off 4 sts at beg of next 2 rows. Cast off rem 11 sts.

(c) Front border

Work as given for waistcoat.

(c) To make up

Press as given for sweater. Join shoulder and sleeve seams. Set in sleeves. Turn hems at lower edge and cuffs to WS and sl st down. Sew on front border. Press seams. Sew on buttons.

Reference section

General knitting abbreviations

alt	alternate(ly)	P	purl
approx	approximate(ly)	P-wise	purlwise direction
beg	begin(ning)	rem	remain(ing)
cm	centimetre	rep	repeat(ing)
cont	continu(e)(ing)	R S	right side of work
dec	decreas(e)(ing)	sl	slip
foll	follow(ing)	sl st	slip stitch
g st	garter stitch	st(s)	stitch(es)
g	gramme(s)	st st	stocking stitch
inc	increas(e)(ing)	tbl	through back of loop
K	knit	tog	together
K up	pick up and knit	W S	wrong side of work
K-wise	knitwise direction	ybk	yarn back
mm	millimetre(s)	yfwd	yarn forward
psso	pass slipped stitch over	yon	yarn over needle
patt	pattern	yrn	yarn round needle

List of spinners' addresses

If you experience difficulty in obtaining any
of the yarns given in this book, please write
direct to the following addresses:

Emu yarns
Emu Ltd,
Leeds Road,
Greengates,
Bradford BD10 9TE, Yorks.

Hayfield yarns
Hayfield Textiles Ltd,
Hayfield Mills,
Glusburn,
Keighley BD20 8QP, W. Yorks.

Lee Target yarns
George Lee & Sons,
P.O. Box 37,
Wakefield, Yorks.

Lister yarns
Lister & Co.,
P.O. Box 37,
Providence Mills,
Wakefield, Yorks.

Patons yarns
Patons and Baldwins Ltd,
P.O. Box,
Darlington, Co. Durham.

Robin yarns
Robin Wools Ltd,
Robin Mills,
Idle,
Bradford BD10 9TE, Yorks.

Sirdar yarns
Sirdar Ltd,
P.O. Box 31,
Alverthorpe,
Wakefield WF2 9ND, Yorks.

Sunbeam yarns
Richard Ingham & Co. Ltd,
Crawshaw Mills,
Pudsey LS28 7BS, Yorks.

3 Suisses yarns
Filature de l'Espierres,
13, Saffron Way,
Leicester LE2 6UP.

Wendy yarns
Carter & Parker Ltd,
Gordon Mills,
Netherfield Road,
Guiseley LS20 9PD, Yorks.

Further reading

Dawson, Pam, *Knitting Fashion*, B B C Publications, 1976

Dawson, Pam, *A Complete Guide to Knitting*, Marshall Cavendish, 1976

Phillips, Mary Walker, *Creative Knitting*, Van Nostrand Reinhold, 1972

Thomas, Mary, *A Book of Knitting Patterns*, Hodder & Stoughton, 1943

Thomas, Mary, *A Knitting Book*, Hodder & Stoughton, 1938

Walker, Barbara G., *A Treasury of Knitting Patterns*, Pitman Publishing, 1968

Walker, Barbara G., *A Second Treasury of Knitting Patterns*, Pitman Publishing, 1971